GUY MADDIN'S
**MY WINNIPEG**

Guy Maddin is Canada's most iconoclastic filmmaker. Through his rein-
vention of half-forgotten film genres, his use of abandoned techniques
from the early history of cinema, and his unique editing style, Maddin
has created a critically successful body of work that looks like nothing
else in Canadian film. *My Winnipeg* (2008) has consolidated Maddin's
international reputation.

In this sixth volume of the Canadian Cinema series, Darren Wershler
argues that Maddin's use of techniques and media that fall outside of
the normal repertoire of contemporary cinema requires us to re-exam-
ine what we think we know about the documentary genre and even
'film' itself. Through an exploration of *My Winnipeg*'s major thematic
concerns – memory, the cultural archive, and how people and objects
circulate through the space of the city – Wershler contends that the
result is a film that is psychologically and affectively true without being
historically accurate.

DARREN WERSHLER is an assistant professor in the Department of English
at Concordia University.

CANADIAN CINEMA 6

# GUY MADDIN'S
## MY WINNIPEG

**DARREN WERSHLER**

UNIVERSITY OF TORONTO PRESS
Toronto Buffalo London

tiff.

© University of Toronto Press Incorporated 2010
Toronto Buffalo London
www.utppublishing.com
Printed in Canada

ISBN: 978-1-4426-4246-1 (cloth)
ISBN: 978-1-4426-1134-4 (paper)

Printed on acid-free and 100% post-consumer recycled paper with
vegetable-based inks.

---

**Library and Archives Canada Cataloguing in Publication**

Wershler-Henry, Darren S. (Darren Sean), 1966–
Guy Maddin's My Winnipeg / Darren Wershler.

(Canadian cinema ; 6)
Includes bibliographical references.
ISBN 978-1-4426-4246-1 (bound)      ISBN 978-1-4426-1134-4 (pbk.)

1. Maddin, Guy – Criticism and interpretation.    2. My Winnipeg
(Motion picture).    I. Title.    II. Title: My Winnipeg.    III. Series:
Canadian cinema (Toronto, Ont.) ; 6.

PN1997.2.M92W47 2010      791.430233092      C2010-904590-4

---

TIFF and the University of Toronto Press acknowledge the financial
assistance to its publishing program of the Canada Council for the Arts
and the Ontario Arts Council.

  Canada Council    Conseil des Arts        ONTARIO ARTS COUNCIL
for the Arts      du Canada           CONSEIL DES ARTS DE L'ONTARIO

This book has been published with the help of a grant from the Canadian
Federation for the Humanities and Social Sciences, through the Aid
to Scholarly Publications Program, using funds provided by the Social
Sciences and Humanities Research Council of Canada.

University of Toronto Press acknowledges the financial support for its
publishing activities of the Government of Canada through the Book
Publishing Industry Development Program (BPIDP).

For my mom, Frances Wershler (nee Lowes),
Winnipeg Salad Queen, July 1964

Memory is not an instrument for exploring the past but its theater. It is the medium of past experience, just as the earth is the medium in which dead cities lie buried.

– Walter Benjamin, 'Berlin Chronicle'

# Contents

1  Breaking and Entering: An Introduction                    3

2  Transfusions: Biography and Filmography                   16

3  The Peculiar Enchantments of Winnipeg:
   The Commission                                            37

4  A Glorious Dress-up Chest: Genre                          52

5  More Ellipses: The City and Circulation                  66

6  The Forks beneath the Forks: Desire and Drive            86

7  Goat-Glanding and Other Delights:
   Narration and Sound                                       97

8  Viscous and Cottony Hallucinations:
   Memory and Haunted Media                                 103

9  Beautifully Broken: Conclusions                          117


*Production Credits*                                        121
*Further Viewing*                                           125
*Notes*                                                     127
*Bibliography*                                              137

GUY MADDIN'S
**MY WINNIPEG**

# Breaking and Entering:
# An Introduction

The unfeeling coroner's chisel breaks in the bones at the temples, gets at the
memories.

– Guy Maddin, narration for *My Winnipeg*

'I receive almost no visits from dead loved ones in my dreams,' says
Guy Maddin. 'It's just empty architecture for me every night.'[1] In his
dreams, the director of *My Winnipeg* wanders through ramshackle structures abandoned by all living things, 'but still somehow packed with
love, with sadness, with something latent.'[2]

One of the reasons that Maddin's films are compelling is that, like
the abandoned and condemned buildings in his dreams, they offer a
range of possible entry points. In his book *Kino Delirium: The Films of Guy
Maddin*, Caelum Vatnsdal argues that 'a Maddin movie is a gallery of
film references to the cinephile, a picture book of deliciously wild imagery to the aesthete, a minefield of over-the-top dementia to the arm-
chair psychoanalyst, and a fascinating, provocative curio for everyone
else.'[3] The entryways into Maddin's films are not only thematic but,
as is the case with many other contemporary films, are also variations
in material form. The specific manner in which *My Winnipeg* and Maddin's other recent films constitute what might be called a 'differential
cinema' is one of the major concerns of this book.

As Toby Miller has pointed out, the brief period in the mid-twentieth century when the process of going to the theatre to watch a celluloid film might have led scholars to think of cinema as a unitary phenomenon is long over.[4] Victor Burgin's *In/Different Spaces* outlines the many ways in which a 'film' is once again no longer a coherent object, but an assemblage:

> a 'film' may be encountered through posters, 'blurbs,' and other advertisements, such as trailers and television clips; it may be encountered through newspaper reviews, reference work synopses and theoretical articles (with their 'film-strip' assemblages of still images); through production photographs, frame enlargements, memorabilia and so on .... Clearly this 'film' – a heterogeneous psychical object, constructed from image scraps scattered in space and time – is a very different object from that encountered in the context of 'film studies.'[5]

To this list of objects that were arguably always part of cinema, even if they were largely ignored, we could add a number of specifically digital objects: clips on YouTube and other video portals; films streamed to our smartphones and tablets from remote servers; official film websites; DVDs with special features, commentaries, alternative endings, out-takes and other kinds of supplementary materials; video on demand through the Xbox Network; pirated versions, often of screeners or rough cuts, available over UseNet or BitTorrent (as of this writing, even after the demise of the Pirate Bay, there are several active torrents of *My Winnipeg*). Maddin himself uploads all of his short films to YouTube. 'My distributors take them down now and then,' he says. 'I love my distributors, but I kinda think that shorts should be out there, even if I have to pirate them myself.'[6] In sum, Burgin notes, the 'classic' narrative film became the object of film studies only by ignoring the space 'around' the film that is 'formed from all of the many places of transition between cinema and other images in and of everyday life.'[7] In 2010 it is no longer possible to ignore those places of transition; film studies and media studies have to take them into account.

Part of the answer to why this is the case lies in how we know what we know about some of the ghostly buildings of Maddin's dreams. Two buildings figure prominently in this imaginary landscape. One is the former Lil's Beauty Shop at 800 Ellice Avenue, now partitioned into a set of apartments. Run by Maddin's aunt, Lil Eyolfson, and his mother, Herdis Maddin, 800 Ellice was also the Maddin family home. The other is the now demolished Winnipeg Arena, where Maddin's father, Chas, worked as the manager of the Winnipeg Maroons. Between the memories of these two structures, *My Winnipeg* shuttles back and forth like the ghost of one of Winnipeg's long-since vanished streetcars.

If Winnipeg has a public body, then for Maddin, the Winnipeg Arena was its head. 'For fifty years, this ice-hockey cathedral fit Winnipeg and its sport like a skull fits its brain,' intones the narrator. This phrase is also a kind of ghost. It previously appeared in 'The Child without Qualities,' a treatment in *From the Atelier Tovar: Selected Writings* that contains many elements of *My Winnipeg* and the two other films in Maddin's autobiographical 'Me Trilogy,' *Cowards Bend the Knee* (2003) and *Brand Upon the Brain!* (2006), and echoes through a wide range of Maddin's interviews. Yet Vatnsdal notes that as late as 2000 Maddin still had no intention of expanding or producing 'The Child without Qualities.'[8] In the treatment, not only was the Arena 'peopled with lurid throngs somehow cultivated from the film noir grotesques of police photographer Weegee,' but it was filled with 'thick clouds' of cigarette smoke, which 'often billowed down to ice level, where the elevated, celebrity criminals were forced to play their game with much confusion and bluffing about where the puck, or pucks, and other players (everything lost in the nebulous exhalations) actually were.'[9] A skull full of smoke, populated by noir extras: a perfect image for the sensibility that informs Maddin's work, especially *Cowards Bend the Knee*. In *My Winnipeg*, not even the outline remains – only its memory. Magically, the smoke-filled head becomes a broken, bleeding heart: 'my building lies like a heart ripped open in the snow.'

In stark contrast to the 16mm black and white footage that makes up most of the rest of *My Winnipeg*, Maddin has captured the demolition of the Winnipeg Arena in colour video. As Maddin sneaks into a forbidden area of the demolition site to pee in the Arena men's room's infamous urinal trough for the last time, wearing a hard hat instead of the helmet-like coatings of Brylcreem favoured by his childhood hockey heroes, the narrator waxes metaphysical: 'The unfeeling coroner's chisel breaks in the bones at the temples, gets at the memories.' Those memories are about origins. For the Child without Qualities, 'The Winnipeg Arena seems like the only home once one is actually inside it.'[10] For the narrator of *My Winnipeg*, 'This building was my male parent, and everything male in my childhood I picked up right here.' It has its own unique bouquet of smells ('Urine. Breast milk. Sweat') and its own erotic charge. The narrator describes his younger self first encountering nude Soviet superstar Anatoli Firsov in the shower room, then later stealing his sweater and slipping it over his nude body, nearly fainting 'from the touch of its fabric and the fear.' As with most stories of origins, the narrative quickly becomes myth: 'I was even born right here in this dressing room.' There are many such myths, exaggerations, factual errors and outright lies in *My Winnipeg*. However, this isn't a Peter Greenaway film. The point isn't to enumerate and evaluate the anachronisms and continuity errors, deliberate or otherwise, but to consider how such claims and, in many cases, their opposite counter-claims together create a film that is psychologically and affectively true without being historically accurate.

Maddin's counterpoint to the Winnipeg Arena is the 'big cube of home' at 800 Ellice. Here too, the air is murky and indistinct, 'cloudy,

The demolition of the Winnipeg Arena. Courtesy of Guy Maddin, from the director's personal collection.

Herdis Maddin in a print ad for Lil's. Courtesy of Guy Maddin, from the director's personal collection.

cloudy, cloudy with hairsprays.' Here too, the denizens wear helmets – the hoods of the hair dryers, and the lacquered beehive hairdos that the salon produces. In place of the trough that carries off men's urine is a chute that carries clumps of cut hair down to the basement, and an air vent that carries snatches of gossip up to Guy's bedroom. It too has its signature smells, 'the smells of female vanity and desperation,' and its own eroticism, linked to Maddin's childhood habit of climbing up the inside of the hair chute to spy on women's legs from the trap door.[11] Where the Arena is male, 800 Ellice is a 'gynocracy.'

Even this brief exploration of two of the settings of *My Winnipeg* requires reference to several objects other than the film proper: the published edition of the annotated script, several interviews, and an older film treatment in Maddin's selected writings. Over the course of this book, this assemblage of references will grow even thicker, like one of the matted clumps of hair from the chute in the floor of the salon at 800 Ellice. These issues hold even for films that do *not* take fragmentation and the cultural archive as their explicit subject matter as *My Winnipeg* does. It is simply easier to see in the case of a film like this one.

Burgin uses Foucault's term 'heterotopia' to describe this juxtaposition of supposedly incommensurable elements in cinema,[12] but I prefer Marjorie Perloff's notion of 'differential media.' Perloff's term retains its focus on media and mediality, whereas 'heterotopia' connotes a particular kind of space, like Augé's 'non-place.'[13]Perloff developed the notion of differential media in 2000 to describe Kenneth Goldsmith's *Fidget*, which is, variously, a musical score, several professionally tailored paper suits, a Web-based Java application, a pair of large visual poems on paper, a performance piece, and a book. Further, these heterogeneous objects are not subsumed into the totality of the book; no one object in the assemblage dominates.

The important distinction between differential media and more established terms such as 'intermedia' and 'transmedia,' then, is that differential media describes an assemblage where no element necessarily takes priority over any other. Intermedia, in the sense that Dick Higgins popularized it in the mid-1960s,[14] describes a work that incorporates more than one media form. Maddin's *Dracula: Pages from a Virgin's Diary*, which is a hybrid of ballet and cinema, would be an example of intermedia in Higgins's sense. Gene Youngblood's use of 'intermedia' in the later 1960s to describe the network of 'cinema, television, radio, magazines, books, and newspapers' that constitutes the total environment in which the meaning of a given cultural object is established[14] describes a context rather than an object of study, so it is not particularly helpful for the purposes of describing Maddin's work. Nor does Henry Jenkins's notion of 'transmedia' quite fit in this context, because its focus on 'the flow of content across multiple media channels' describes the way that corporate entertainment networks franchise content outward from a property such as a Hollywood film for use in video games, novelizations, and other licensed products.[15] A work such as *Fidget* or *My Winnipeg*, on the other hand, exists simultaneously and '*differentially* in alternate media, as if to say that knowledge is now available through different channels and by different means.'[16] Thinking about *My Winnipeg* necessarily involves the film (with and without live narration), but also the book, the DVD and its various related short films and commentary tracks, the official website, links between this film and Maddin's two other autobiographical films, his two books, and an installation at the Power Plant, without either attributing symmetry between various versions of the object or assigning primacy to any particular one of them.

The boundaries of *My Winnipeg* extend across more than the space between material media; they also extend across time. Just as the spectral buildings of Maddin's dreams create an unresolvable spatial tension – *where* is home? – they also define an irresolvable temporal tension – *when* is home? In his annotations to the script of *My Winnipeg*,

Maddin provides a gloss for his description of the city as the sleep-walking capital of the world, positioning its citizens as existing in a temporal confusion to match the spatial one he has already delineated: 'We Winnipeggers visit the cityscapes of both worlds, the past and the present, which exist contemporaneously. The people and buildings that were once here but are now gone are allowed to coexist with those that remain. We remember equally what happened today and long ago: no temporal distinction is made, and therefore no qualitative distinction either.'[17]

Raymond Williams famously describes this specific sort of relationship to elements of one's cultural past as *residual*. He writes, 'The residual, by definition, has been effectively formed in the past, but it is still active in the cultural process, not only and often not at all as an element of the past, but as an effective element of the present.' For Williams, the residual is different from the merely archaic in that it sticks out somehow from the dominant culture, and may go so far as to present an 'alternative or even oppositional relation' to it, laying the groundwork for the possible dialectical appearance of 'emergent' cultural forms.[19] However, as Charles Acland points out in the introduction to his recent collection *Residual Media*, the distance between dominant and residual is often 'razor thin,'[20] resulting in what might be described as a '"living dead" culture'[21] – not so far from Maddin's city of indifferent sleepwalkers. Williams warns that it is quite possible to mistake 'the locally residual (as a form of resistance to incorporation)' for the genuinely emergent. For Acland, this is particularly true now that various forms of analogue and digital storage media have changed our relationship to the past by ensuring that 'things and practices hang around long past their supposed use-by date.'[22] Acland calls for a renewed analysis of the role that the circulation and transformation of the residual plays in the ongoing production of culture because only such a process will help us to determine what we want to happen next.

When we think about Maddin's films, it is necessary to consider the question of material form in terms of both their continuities with and differences from historically specific styles and genres. In his essay on Maddin's *Careful,* Will Straw explains that the director's chief points of reference are 'the lost codes of late-silent/early-sound cinema, 'deployed in an artisanal 'painstaking reconstruction' of obscure past film styles.'[23] 'Painstaking' is the *mot juste* here, as the example of *Careful* amply demonstrates. Maddin describes the visual style of this film, which evokes the aesthetics of the 1920s German *bergfilme* ('mountain films') of director Arnold Fanck and others, as 'fragile Repress-O-Vision' (look for the 2009 DVD re-release with the colour newly muted to the director's satisfaction). It turns out that Repress-O-Vision has a very specific recipe: 'overexposing one to three stops and then having the lab print it back down gave us the repressed saturation that we liked. Plus the blow-up technology of 1992 still took a little more off the film, added a little more grain.' Maddin also used a variety of effects, ranging from fog filters to shooting through his landlord's window screens to achieve the desired effects.[24] Attention to the interrelation of style, genre, and medium generates a reading that's much more versatile and more compelling than Steven Shaviro's claim that the stylistic elements of Maddin's films 'are entirely non-functional' and 'have nothing beyond themselves to express,' but are merely part of a 'cinema of spectacle.'[25]

Nevertheless, all of this painstaking labour does *not* result in the construction of a film that could just as easily have been made in 1928. Again, Straw is helpful on this point: 'Maddin's films are both inventive revisitings of genuine past styles and imagined versions of such styles.'[26] A.O. Scott concurs: '[Maddin's] enthusiasm for obsolescent cinematic techniques – silent-film emoting, iris lenses, shadowy monochrome, collagist editing – is at once antiquarian and futuristic, a way of exhuming buried possibilities for novelty and speculation.'[27] By resorting to these specific but forgotten residual cinematic techniques, Maddin attempts to build an emergent cinema for the future. Along the way, he eschews most of the trappings of nostalgia by *not* filming his past as though it were some tranquil little world cordoned off from the rest of history. What does it mean, exactly, for a director to film the 1950s as though they were the 1920s?

Learning the audiovisual vocabulary of the cinema of decades past also requires access to some sort of archive, which, in turn, raises all sorts of questions about the assumptions of historical accuracy we usually make when dealing with archives. Maddin owns 160 16mm films that were the former core of the University of Manitoba film studies program library. He simply picked them up from the curbside when the university was going to throw them out. Many (perhaps even most) of these prints are duplicates, made by a U.S. distributor who routinely copied what came through the obscure northern market of Winnipeg. Maddin describes how, as a result of viewing this library of multiple-generation copies, he developed a visual aesthetic that was effectively a function of piracy:

> I drew all the delightfully wrong conclusions about what old films are supposed to look like. I thought they were high-contrast because they were old, but they're high-contrast because they're duplicates of duplicates of duplicates. If you've ever photocopied things until you get just black and white, that's what they are. It's because of the economy in duplicated, pirated prints that *Pandora's Box*, an already high-contrast movie, looks like a photocopy in some prints that are circulating around.[28]

'Circulating' is the key word here; in addition to the issues already outlined above, we also need to be thinking about how objects, texts, and bodies move through the circuits of culture and what happens to them as they do.

Dilip Gaonkar and Elizabeth Povinelli, whose essay 'Technologies of

Public Forms' is a key document in the nascent theory of circulation, make a case for the value of describing the cultures of circulation within which forms, texts, events, and practices emerge and how they are 'transfigured' as they move into situations where they are put to a variety of different ends.[29] Gaonkar and Povinelli's interest is in the places where people, cultural objects, discourses, and other forms touch and interact – their 'edges' or interfaces – because, as Straw remarks in his paper 'The Circulatory Turn,' these interfaces are what determines an object's mobility. Straw also notes that this form of study is particularly compelling when one considers cultural ephemera in an urban setting, because focusing on a single object 'is less interesting than the remapping of the city which goes on as the edges of these things join together in series or pathways. To study the "edges of forms" is to study not only the containers of meaning, but the systems of assembly and interconnection which give texture to urban cultural life.'[30]

Circulation theory is ideally suited to serve as a framework for discussing a film about a city. In addition to questions of media, form, and genre, this book also deals with aspects of *My Winnipeg*'s circulation: the specific but diverse material qualities of movies in a networked digital milieu; the changing rhetoric of nationalism around art made in Canada and its putative 'Canadianness'; the people and agencies responsible for the film's inception and the economics of creativity in independent Canadian film; Maddin's transfiguration of older film genres for his own ends; his changing attitude towards the filmmaking process; the implications of the shift from a modern to a postmodern milieu for film criticism; the shifting nature of the city symphony as a genre; and the circulation and production of narratives about Winnipeg via historical documents and conversations with friends.

But this is still not the only form of circulation that needs to be taken into account when addressing *My Winnipeg*, because it is a film that is deeply concerned with questions of desire and drive – how they flow, how they are blocked, and how the former can paper over the latter in ways that are particularly problematic. When we attempt to address this level of circulation in Maddin's work, Slavoj Žižek's unique combination of philosophy, Lacanian psychoanalysis, and film criticism is extremely useful to have in the critical mix. Of crucial importance is what Žižek refers to as 'the ethic of drive.' In Lacanian psychoanalysis, the job of fantasy is to create a narrative that covers up some sort of original deadlock.[31] As already suggested, *My Winnipeg* is built largely around such deadlocks: the irreconcilability of maternal and paternal spaces, of the past glories of Winnipeg and its entropic present, and of the spiritual and the physical. Overwhelmed, the narrator's first response is to fantasize about fleeing the city by train, something he has tried before and has always failed to accomplish. Overcoming such dilemmas requires something that might at first seem counter-intuitive: in order to move past ('traverse') the fantasy, it is necessary to embrace the traumatic, impossible force that lurks beneath it ... in this case, the force 'as strong as all the trains in Manitoba': Mother.

Traversing the fantasy in this manner also has interesting implications for the way that we conventionally think about the genre of documentary. Žižek explains: 'The point is *not* to remember the past trauma as exactly as possible: such "documentation" is a priori false, it transforms the trauma into a neutral, objective fact, whereas the essence of the trauma is precisely that it is too horrible to be remembered, to be integrated into our symbolic universe. All we have to do is mark repeatedly the trauma as such ... by means of some 'empty' symbolic gesture.[32] Many documentaries claim to be a repository of facts, but Maddin's is a repository of fantasies, a trip through the various ways that he and his city have attempted to hide the traumas that threaten them.

# Transfusions:
# Biography and Filmography

I don't care about historical accuracy.

– Guy Maddin, email to Andy Smetanka[1]

One of Guy Maddin's frequent claims is that Canadians in general and Winnipeggers in particular are poor at remembering, let alone mythologizing, our own history.[2] From Maddin's perspective, this shortcoming is problematic because thinking through the inextricable and often contradictory tangle of past events and personal fantasy is precisely what leads to a greater sense of *psychological* truth.[3] *How* we remember is as important as *what* we remember.

The way that Maddin remembers his birth is a case in point. Guy Maddin was born in Winnipeg on 28 February 1956, but that flake of autobiographical certitude soon vanishes in a blizzard of embellishment. In the annotated script of *My Winnipeg*, he claims that he was born on 'the very day that television broadcasting began in Winnipeg, and I was brought home from the hospital the same day as our new TV set.'[4] The historical record shows that CBWT, the Canadian Broadcasting Corporation's Winnipeg television station, began beaming out its signal to nearby homes almost two years earlier, on Tuesday, 1 June 1954.[5] Nevertheless, Maddin's imaginary linking of his birth to the first appearance of local TV is more significant for our purposes than the facts.

Maddin's narrative of his ongoing relationship to the TV quickly develops a decidedly erotic quality: 'It wasn't till my sister noticed one of us masturbating in front of the unblinking stare of the other that our perhaps too-close relationship was called into question.'[6] The ambiguity over which party is watching and which is masturbating is humorous, but it also points to the *imaginary* character of Maddin's aesthetic, particularly the films in which characters named 'Guy Maddin' appear. In Lacanian accounts of subject formation, the subject's encounter with its mirror image is characterized by a particular kind of horror. The mediated image always lacks a certain undefinable 'something' that makes it different than oneself – in a word, uncanny. Further, as Slavoj Žižek points out, doubles have a nasty habit of switching positions. Instead of experiencing our double as radically other, we instead recognize ourselves in our uncanny, empty copy. The price to be paid for maintaining a consistent sense of self is to experience ourselves as the empty, loathsome Things at the point of the gaze. Žižek suggests that rather than trying to settle on one version or the other as verisimilar, a more fruitful approach is to focus instead on the conditions and spaces that allow such ambiguous figures to appear.[7] The doppelgängers that populate Maddin's films are indolent cowards, mama's boys, philanderers, and murderers. What is interesting is not whether these figures are somehow 'accurate' reflections of the director's personality, but how Maddin uses them to display his fantasies onscreen.

Maddin also uses the narrative of his preschool 'symbiotic friendship' with the television as a framing device for a lifelong concern not simply with the content of media, but also with its formal and material qualities. 'I basically just studied the television, or the test pattern before television went on in the morning, or, before that, the snow,' Maddin tells Caelum Vatnsdal. 'I'd sit and watch the snowy transmissions just to get five seconds of clear, illicit Amercian television. I guess you might look there for a first trace of an apparent love affair with degraded imagery, or with veils or mists or blizzards of decomposition in front of them.'[8] The normative balance of signal and noise is inverted here. Maddin watches more noise than signal, and when the signal does arrive, it is somehow 'illicit.' For Maddin, the qualities of media are thus never neutral; they always have a geographical and political specificity to them. Even a toddler, he claims, could tell a Canadian television show from an American one because of the former's 'lousy lighting and acoustics.'[9]

In the considerable number of interviews he has conducted since the beginning of his directorial career, Maddin's narrative of his childhood and adolescence invariably returns to his fascination with the formal qualities of media, especially with the aspect that most people try to ignore: the noise and interference. Maddin's foregrounding of media noise occurs not only around television, but around other forms of electromechanical media as well. 'The Child without Qualities' describes the Child's older brother Cameron Bellamy using 'a tubecrammed, stove-size reel-to-reel tape recorder' to capture the 'ever-so-distant' voices on a transatlantic telephone call, where the operator 'shouts weakly like a woman drowning amidst an audio tempest' of 'the clunks, drone and whistles attending all such iron-curtain cable-calls.' For the listeners, the source might well be 'a lot further away than the deathly Czechoslovakia, as if the cable ended somewhere in a grave, as if the ghostly transmission were from a far corner of heaven, a heaven of grimy ghettoes.'[10] The treatment's explicit suggestion is that communication is always 'miscommunication,' presenting, as John Durham Peters writes, a 'vision of communication, in any setting, as essentially communication with the dead: never as the touching of consciousness, only as the interpretation of traces.'[11]

Listening to the radio plays a particularly important role in the way Maddin describes the development of his aesthetic:

I'm kind of an obsessive, and as a kid I became obsessed with baseball broadcasts from very distant American AM radio stations for a while. Listening to them is like listening to secret CIA short-wave 'casts – they're very layered with interferences from other stations, or percussive signals from satellites or something. It's like listening to sound sculpture, and every now and then a pitch count, or a play-by-play announcer's voice would weave in throughout all of the layers of static and crackle and give a little bit of desperately needed information before weaving off into the distance again. Since the reinforcement was so intermittent I really got hooked on listening to this stuff in my loneliest, most virginal, deepest darkest adolescent days. I sort of constructed, in the isolation of Winnipeg, this model, almost like a blind person would, of what America looked like, based on the acoustic landscape I got from these things.[12]

In *Listening In: Radio and the American Imagination*, Susan J. Douglas describes this practice of listening for distant radio stations, or 'DXing,' as central to the development of a sense of romance and mystery around radio as a medium, of modern notions of masculinity and its attendant assumption of technological mastery, of the prurient pleasures of eavesdropping, and of the differences wrought by cultural regionalism and nationalism.[13] Though the period Douglas describes is the formative period of radio listening – the early 1920s, a good forty years before Maddin's childhood radio days – it is somehow appropriate that he had adopted radio-listening patterns characteristic of the decade he would come to fetishize as a filmmaker. The other major difference between Douglas's DXers and Maddin is that, while the former did their best to enjoy radio listening despite the 'maddening' interference, Maddin describes enjoying radio partly *because* of it. This inseparability of signal and noise and, for that matter, of the rational and the irrational, would become a hallmark of Maddin's aesthetic.

Nazis burning Guy Maddin's Math and Economics textbooks. Courtesy of Guy Maddin, from the director's personal collection.

Despite his vividly imaginary, media-saturated childhood, Maddin's graduation from high school marked the beginning of his 'left-hemisphere days' as student of mathematics and economics at the University of Manitoba. Maddin claims that the books that the Nazis burn in the 'If Day' sequence of *My Winnipeg* are leftover calculus textbooks from this period.[14] After the break-up of his first marriage and subsequent leaving of his unhappy employment as a bank teller, Maddin began painting houses for a living. He occasionally invokes this part of his résumé in order to contrast his own aesthetic with that of the unabashedly elitist painter-director Peter Greenaway.[15] More important, Maddin began auditing the film classes that his 'old Marxist pal,' Bob Nixon, was taking at the University of Manitoba. Nixon, along with Noam Gonick and Jonah Corne, would eventually be one of the friends who helped Maddin most on *My Winnipeg*, 'supplying me in preproduction with a steady stream of half-and-mis-remembered local myths.'[16] Soon, Maddin was giving rides home to the class professor, George Toles, who would eventually become Maddin's screenwriting partner on the majority of his films.

Before he became a filmmaker, Maddin had a brief but varied acting career, building on even earlier experience as a child model for the Hudson's Bay Company. Few people outside Winnipeg have heard of (let alone seen) Maddin and Greg Klymkiw's VPW public access cable TV's mock-talk show *S\*U\*R\*V\*I\*V\*A\*L*, but it was a cult favourite during the early 1980s. In 1982 *S\*U\*R\*V\*I\*V\*A\*L* even spawned a novelty song by Winnipeg punk group 4 Men with Sight called 'Kill the Mutants,' which received some airplay on 92-CITI FM, the local album-oriented rock station. Alongside his camouflage-masked roommate Klymkiw, as the show's violently sociopathic host, 'Trevor Winthrop-Baines,' Maddin played a befuddled, bandanna-wearing sidekick named 'Concerned Citizen Stan.' Following the ear-splitting screech of Klymkiw's signature opening rant ('WEEEE MUST SURVIVE THE INEVITABLE SOCIO-

ECONOMIC COLLAPSE AND/OR NUCLEAR HOLOCAUST!'), the two
and their occasional guests spent the remainder of each episode discussing the ins and outs of properly stocking a bomb shelter and surviving
attacks from radioactive mutants. Maddin also had a number of small
film roles, beginning as an extra in *Silence of the North* (1979), starring El-
len Burstyn.[17] He later appeared in two of John Paizs's short movies for
the Winnipeg Film Group, including roles as a student in *Oak, Ivy, and
Other Dead Elms* (1982) and as a homicidal nurse in *The International Style*
(1984).[18] More recently, he appeared in actor-director Caelum Vatnsdal's
*Black as Hell, Strong as Death, Sweet as Love* (1998), reciprocating for Vatnsdal's turn as Osip in Maddin's acclaimed short film *The Heart of the World.*

One of Maddin's occcupations outside the world of film is significant, especially in the context of the discussion of a film like *My Winnipeg*. By 1988, when he was making his first feature, *Tales from the Gimli
Hospital*, Maddin had a day job as a photo archivist at the Manitoba pro-
vincial records depository. This experience not only exposed the young
director to a vast array of historical materials, but it also allowed him
to develop a fairly keen sense of the relation of the material qualities
of photographic media to specific historical periods. 'I got really good
at dating pictures,' Maddin tells Caelum Vatnsdal in an interview for
*Kino Delirium: The Films of Guy Maddin*. 'I could date a photo to sometimes within a month of when it was taken, using the photo stock and
paper as well as seasonal clues and a knowledge of Winnipeg history.
Sometimes I'd get really cocky and guess the day, and a few times I was
right.'[19]

Nevertheless, an artist's research is not the same as an archivist's, because the two have very different agendas. Poets bpNichol and Steve Mc-
Caffery make a distinction between artistic and scholarly research that
illustrates the point nicely. Artistic research, which locates, describes,
and analyses obscure but nevertheless exciting texts, is uninterested in
making the sorts of claims to professional legitimacy or academic rigour

that scholarly research makes. The aim of artistic research is to articulate a particular point of view in a way that is associative as well as historical and logical. For those who choose to investigate further, it offers a starting point, but not prescriptive conclusions.[20] When one is considering how to approach the oeuvre of a filmmaker like Maddin, who is not only conversant with a huge range of forgotten historical forms and professionally trained in how to ferret out archival materials, yet disarmingly casual about historical accuracy, the idea of artistic research is a useful notion.

Maddin himself describes his artistic research as a kind of vampirism. 'I have this little fantasy where I go back in time and steal films from other directors to assemble a great filmography for myself. But it's like taking a blood transfusion: you don't want to take enough to kill them, or even stagger them, but some amount that benefits you while leaving them plenty of blood to live.'[21] This oddly humble daydream of draining away the lesser films of his favourite directors is an apt allegory for artistic influence. What it obscures, though, is that somewhere off in the dark corners of various underutilized Winnipeg warehouses, he has already created a vivid celluloid corpus of his own.

Since 1985 Maddin has directed seven features and an astonishing twenty-six short films, not including various incomplete, abandoned, and disowned works. In 2009 Maddin was one of a dozen people named to the Order of Manitoba. His national and international reputation grows with each new release, bringing prizes and accolades from film festivals around the world. Though Maddin has joked that 'all Canadian movies *should* look alike; it's kind of a team uniform,'[22] his audiovisual style is instantly recognizable because of its singularity. Roger Ebert, a long-time fan of Maddin, recently wrote that 'shot for shot, Maddin can be as surprising and delightful as any filmmaker has ever been.'[23] Given that it is still early in Maddin's career and that *My Winnipeg* has resulted in his most positive reviews and greatest level of attention to date, it is reasonable to expect that he holds further odd and lurid novelties in store.

Philosopher and film critic Slavoj Žižek argues that the only way to make something truly new is by a particular kind of repetition. What is repeated in such a moment is not how the past 'actually was,' but is rather an unused reservoir of potential that was never fully tapped.[24] Artist, filmmaker, and academic Renée Green makes a similar argument about memory: when we think of it as an active process rather than 'a form of entombment,' it allows for the development of a relationship with the past that permits continual reconsideration of what older forms might do for us now.[25] Because of his ongoing resuscitation of the film genres of the past, especially those of the 1920s – the melodrama, the partial talkie, the mountain film, the city symphony – and retrofitting them for his own purposes, Maddin's work can be difficult to classify in terms of conventional contemporary notions of genre. For an independent Canadian filmmaker, this approach has economic implications that are inseparable from the aesthetic issues it raises. In an interview with Michael Ondaatje, Maddin dryly comments that he stopped thinking his distinctiveness was always an asset when it became obvious that movies that fit a particular genre are much easier to market.[26]

Maddin began his first film, *The Dead Father* (1985), largely at the urging of his longtime friend John Boles Harvie, a bon vivant and silent-film enthusiast. By the time he began shooting, Maddin had seen several of University of Manitoba film professor Steve Snyder's short experimental films and some of the key early works by Surrealists Man Ray and Luis Buñuel.[27] Motivated by the visual equivalent of a 'garage band aesthetic,' Maddin began a process that he thought would end quickly but took three years to complete. Even in this first short work, several themes that run through Maddin's oeuvre are already present: the (partly) dead father, the self-loathing son, and the setting in 'the

Dominion of Forgetfulness.' To this day, Maddin's fictional worlds are populated largely by amnesiacs, somnambulists, and the undead.

The production of Maddin's first feature, *Tales from the Gimli Hospital* (1988), was based on a concept by Ian Handford, Maddin's house-painting buddy and another silent-film lover. Filming took eighteen months and was possible primarily because, when Maddin applied for $9,200 from the Manitoba Arts Council, he was granted the maximum $20,000. Maddin tells Caelum Vatnsdal that the actual cost of the film is open to conjecture. Critics usually describe it as costing the full amount of the grant, 'but I don't know if it cost fourteen thousand or thirty thousand. Somewhere in between there.'[28] The film was infamously excluded from the Toronto Festival of Festivals by critic Piers Handling and famously promoted by New York distributor Ben Barenholtz, who also popularized the early work of David Lynch. Set in the fishing community of Gimli, Manitoba (the home of Maddin's Icelandic ancestors) during the smallpox epidemic of 1876–77, the story focuses on the rivalry of two patients, Einar and Gunnar, who rapidly descend into madness as they vie for the attention of their beautiful nurses. *Tales from the Gimli Hospital* is the first example of Maddin's signature process of creating unique new works via a process that critical politesse might label 'dialectical' but Maddin himself refers to as 'plagiarism.' He has remarked in several interviews that, when he began work on *Tales*, he was attempting to copy Erich von Stroheim's *Greed*.[29] The result, after percolating through Maddin's imagination, is something very different. Ironically, despite the fact that the entire script for *Tales from the Gimli Hospital* consists of five Post-It notes, it remains the only film for which Maddin has received a Genie Award nomination for Best Original Screenplay.[30]

The production of Maddin's sophomore feature, *Archangel* (1990), was much more professional and much less leisurely that its predecessors. The film was shot in thirty-five days (still a lengthy shoot for a professional film, but markedly shorter than Maddin's previous schedules) for a cost of $340–75,000. Again, John Boles Harvie was a major influence on the story (*Archangel*'s protagonist is named after him). Harvie was originally going to produce, co-write and star in the film, but owing to his time commitments as an articling law student, Maddin hired Greg Klymkiw to produce. According to Maddin, Harvie left the project shortly after as a result of his and Klymkiw's mutual dislike of each other.[31] George Toles was fully involved in the screenwriting process as well. He appears in the *Tales* credits as 'Story Consultant,' but Maddin asserts that Toles is absent from the *Archangel* credits because of the ambitions of Greg Klymkiw to market himself as an upcoming auteur-producer and Maddin as auteur-director.[32] The film's vertiginous plot concerns a cascade of mistaken identities. Lt John Boles, an amputee Canadian soldier in the northern Russian town of Archangel during World War I, misidentifies Veronkha as his dead lover, Iris; Philbin, Veronkha's husband, forgets he is married to Iris; Veronkha mistakes Boles for Philbin; melodrama ensues. In order to convey an all-pervasive air of snowbound torpor and amnesia, Maddin actually had the actors hypnotized before shooting several scenes in the film and claims that Kyle McCulloch, who played Boles, has no recollection at all of performing the final scene.[33] Praised for its cinematography and voted Best Experimental Film by the U.S. National Society of Film Critics, *Archangel* remains a critical favourite and is one of the most challenging works in Maddin's filmography.

*Careful* (1992) cost just under $1 million to make, half of which was provided by Telefilm Canada. It builds on *Archangel*'s visual strengths, adding a taut, scandalous narrative, which Maddin variously refers to as either 'pro-incest' or 'pro-repression.' In the alpine village of Tölzbad (a pun on the name of co-writer George Toles, who also appears in the film as the dead Countess Knotkers), everyone speaks in whispers, lines their windows with cotton batting, and stifles all strong emotions in an attempt to stave off an avalanche of the glaciers looming above. Threatening to bring everything down in an incestuous, icy Götterdämmerung are the lust for his mother, Zenaida, of aspiring butler Johann; his fiancée, Klara's, lust for her father, Herr Trotta (who in turn desires Klara's sister Sieglinde); and the hatred of Johann's brother Grigorrs for his mother's former lover, the mysterious Count Knotkers. *Careful* is both Maddin's first colour film and his first movie with a real score. 'I was beginning to run out of safe, public domain music to use anyway,' he adds.[34] *Careful* opened 'Perspectives Canada' at the 1993 Toronto International Festival of Festivals, won the Sudbury Cinéfest Best Canadian Film award in 1992, and is the strongest of Maddin's early films.

1994 began well, as the thirty-nine-year-old Maddin became the youngest person ever to win the Telluride Film Festival's Lifetime Achievement Award (placing him in such august company as Leni Riefenstahl, Gloria Swanson, Francis Ford Coppola, Andrei Tarkovsky, and Clint Eastwood). Following that triumph, however, was a long series of disappointments. In 1995 Maddin entered Manitoba's Prairie Waves II screenwriting competition and lost to Gerry Atwell's teleplay *The Hands of Ida*. Maddin was offered a chance to direct it, and, though *The Hands of Ida* (1995) won a Blizzard and was nominated for a Gemini, Maddin has disavowed it and removed it from his filmography. His stated reason for doing so is his lack of satisfaction with the adaptation of the script for filming;[35] the strong family resemblance between *Ida* and *Cowards Bend the Knee* suggests that the latter might even be a kind of 're-boot' of the former. Around the same time, Maddin and Toles had been planning an overly ambitious feature-length project called *The Dikemaster's Daughter*, an operetta based loosely on E.T.A. Hoffmann's *The Sandman* and Theodor Storm's 'Songs of the Dikes.' Maddin had gone so far as to hire an art department and secure a filming location at Gimli before Telefilm withdrew its funding, which amounted to half of the projected budget.[36] An extensive treatment of this elaborate confection, including storyboards and dialogue, was published in *Border Cross-ings* in 1997, after the project had been scrubbed.[37]

Maddin's losing streak was not quite over. *Twilight of the Ice Nymphs* (1997), the first feature that Maddin completed after *Careful*, is the least satisfying of his full-length films both for him and for his critics. Some of the problems were technical. *Twilight* is the only film Maddin has shot in 35mm; he had wanted to use 16mm, but because 1996 was cinema's centennial, Kodak donated the 35mm stock. 'No one really realizes the difference between the two media,' says Maddin, 'and it's hard to put into words, but a painter would tell you there's a big difference between a miniature and a billboard.'[38] At the same time, Maddin also tried to add Dolby Stereo sound, and to expand beyond his usual ensemble of actors to include Hollywood stars such as Frank Gorshin, Shelley Duvall, and Alice Krige – all while dealing with production company Alliance's big-studio demands. Melodrama ensued, but behind the camera rather than in front of it. One quick but telling example is that *Twilight*'s lead actor, Nigel Whitmey, is uncredited, because he removed his name from the marquee after all of his dialogue was over-dubbed by Ross McMillan. In his appendix to the annotated screenplay of *My Winnipeg*, Caelum Vatnsdal candidly calls *Twilight* Maddin's 'most complete failure. Considering it's competing for that title with several movies that were never even finished or released,' he adds, 'that's saying an awful lot.'[39]

Maddin broke the jinx with *The Heart of the World* (2000), the best of his short works and one of his best films, period. Commissioned by the Toronto International Film Festival for its twenty-fifth anniversary along with shorts by nine other name-brand Canadian directors, it was Maddin's first picture at TIFF since 1993. Filmed in the style of Russian Constructivist propaganda, *The Heart of the World* is the story of two brothers ('Nikolai: Youth, Mortician' and 'Osip: An Actor Playing Christ in the Passion Play'), both of whom love and are loved by Anna, 'State Scientist,' who studies the dying, eponymous Heart of the World. Melodrama – and agitprop – follows. Over the next two years, *The Heart of the World* won six major awards, including Best Cinematography at the Aspen Shortfest in 2001 and a Genie for Best Live Action Short Drama in 2002.

*The Heart of the World* marks the onset of a period of increasingly successful feature-length formal experiments for Maddin. Perhaps the most surprising of these is *Dracula: Pages from a Virgin's Diary* (2002), a dance film Maddin made with choreographer Mark Godden and the Royal Winnipeg Ballet for broadcast on the CBC (the film was later released into theatres). Much of *Dracula*'s visceral power derives from the shooting style: Maddin and the other cameramen worked onstage, among the dancers. Maddin tells Michael Ondaatje that 'ballet, when viewed from its centre, is anything but symmetrical and beautiful … You can hear tutus tearing, panties tearing, tendons tearing, and things go in and out of focus because they're moving away from and toward you in chaotic ways.' *Dracula* was the first of Maddin's films on which John Gurdebecke assumed the role of editor instead of Maddin himself. Maddin's collaboration with Gurdebecke is as significant as his writing partnership with George Toles; Maddin considers Gurdebecke 'every bit the filmmaker as the director.'[40] Perceptive critics began to notice that a subtle amalgam of digital and time-honoured analog filmic techniques was brewing in *Dracula*. Bruce Diones wrote in the *New Yorker* that 'Maddin has discovered a new kind of cinema, the welding of silent-film techniques, avant-garde imagery, and twenty-first-century technology (there are digital effects smuggled in throughout the picture).'[41] *Dracula* won ten awards, including the 2002 International Emmy for Arts Programming; Geminis for Best Performing Arts Program and Best Direction in a Performing Arts Program; Best Film at the Sitges-Catalonian International Film Festival; Top Award: Best Screen Choreograph at International Dance Screen, Monaco; and the Grand Prix at International Television Festival Golden Prague.

Following the intermedial *Dracula*, *Cowards Bend the Knee aka The Blue Hands* (2003 installation; 2004 DVD) is Maddin's first true venture into differential media, consisting of an autobiographical book, a series of ten short films installed behind peepholes in the Power Plant Gallery (Toronto, 2003) and at the International Film Festival Rotterdam, and a DVD on which the films can be viewed separately or as a feature. A hockey noir film whose primary settings are the Winnipeg Arena and the Black Silhouette Beauty Salon (actually the name of the salon that rivalled Maddin's Aunt Lil's beauty salon), *Cowards* is the first film in what would eventually become known as Maddin's 'Me Trilogy.' Driven by continual frustration with people saying his films were non-narrative,[42] Maddin crafted a strong story for *Cowards*: 'Boy meets and gets Girl. Boy tries to get rid of Girl. Boy gets what he deserves.'[43] The film stars Darcy Fehr as 'Guy Maddin,' rover for the Winnipeg Maroons. In the seedy backroom clinic of a combination brothel/beauty salon, Guy abandons his girlfriend Veronica mid-abortion to chase the steamy, manipulative Meta, who refuses to let him touch her. During the operation, Veronica dies, only to return as a Ghost working in the brothel/salon. Meta, an Electra figure, attempts to coerce the abortionist (also the Maroons' team doctor) to attach her dead father's preserved hands to Guy's arms. She then convinces Guy to murder her mother Liliom, the brothel's madam and apparent murderer of Chas, her husband and Meta's father. Add a forgotten museum in the rafters of the Winnipeg Arena full of undead waxwork hockey players, a female breast made of ice, visiting Soviets, a rivalry between Guy and his father (the Maroons' play-by-play announcer) for Meta's attentions, and assorted grotesque bit players, and you'll start to get a sense of the film. Again, critics for the most part were kind to *Cowards*. Matt Zoller Seitz of the *New York Press* wrote, 'it feels like a signpost work: a summary of Maddin's techniques and obsessions, a whole life and career packed into 78 minutes.'[44] *Cowards Bend the Knee* won the FIPRESCI Prize – Special Mention at the Rotterdam International Film Festival in 2003.

Based on a screenplay by Kazuo Ishiguro that was exhaustively re-written by Maddin and Toles, *The Saddest Music in the World* (2003) boasted Maddin's biggest budget yet ($2.5 million) and had its debut at the Sundance festival. Starring the formidable Isabella Rossellini as a double-amputee beer magnate with glass *Bierstiefels* (boot-shaped German beer vessels used in elaborate drinking games) for legs, *The Saddest Music in the World* is the first of Maddin's films explicitly set in Winnipeg. The film reinvigorates the musical by populating it with Maddin's now-familiar menagerie of amnesiac nymphomaniacs, depressives bearing preserved relics of their dead loved ones, egotistical heels, and rent boys on the make. Richard Corliss joked in *TIME* that *The Saddest Music in the World* was 'the most enthralling 1933 musical made in 2003.'[45] This is Maddin's most accessible dramatic film and once again it won a stack of awards: the Chlotrudis Award for best Screenplay – Adapted, 2005; the Directors Guild of Canada Craft Award, Outstanding Achievement in Production Design, 2004; and Genies for Best Costume Design, Editing, and Original Score, 2004.

*Brand Upon the Brain!* (2006) is the second and most elaborate of the films in Maddin's 'Me Trilogy.' Dennis Lim describes it as 'an attempt to reinvent the silent film as a full-scale theatrical spectacle.'[46] The Toronto International Film Festival premiere of *Brand* in 2006 featured an eleven-piece orchestra; singer Dov Houle, 'The Manitoba Meadowlark' (an ostensible castrato that Maddin claims to have met in a steam bath in Winnipeg[47]); a five-piece foley artist ensemble; and Maddin as narrator. The film would eventually tour with a series of celebrity interlocutors that Maddin characteristically described as 'Benshi' after the professional Japanese narrrators from Maddin's favourite time period, the 1920s and 1930s. If *Cowards Bend the Knee* is a masochistic and somewhat cynical take on Maddin's childhood, *Brand* is a gentler affair – not without its own suspense and melodramatic moments, but closer to an eroticized Hardy Boys or Nancy Drew tale than the hysterical hoser offspring of film noir and Greek tragedy. In *Brand Upon the Brain!*, house painter 'Guy Maddin' (played by Erik Stephen Maahs as an adult and Sullivan Brown as a boy in flashback sequences) returns as an adult to his parents' orphanage/lighthouse. This spurs a series of flashbacks recalling Guy's boyhood adventures and Shakespearean romantic entanglement with his sister *and* the famous androgynous twin child detectives 'The Lightbulb Kids' as they strive to unravel the secret of the mysterious holes in the back of the orphans' heads. Made entirely with an American cast and crew, *Brand* was the first of Maddin's features to be made outside Winnipeg. It was shot at The Film Company in Seattle, a utopian studio that completely funds the productions of directors that it selects. If, as Fredric Jameson suggests, utopian projects are invariably organized around 'the dismal requirement of failure,'[48] the production of *Brand* was utopian in the truest sense, because the studio ran out of funding for the project while the film was at the lab. Maddin soon found himself trying to finish production on one autobiographical film while simultaneously shooting another one, a film called *My Winnipeg* (2007).

*My Winnipeg* arrived as something of a relief to critics seeking to force a Procrustean fit of Maddin's work into a cinematic canon organized around national identity. In the documentary *97 Percent True*, Maddin is particularly scathing on this point: 'When I first started I'd been watching Canadian film for a long time without much pleasure. Fellow Canadians who remember film watching in the 70s and 80s will remember this unique species of displeasure and shame and second-hand embarrassment we would get watching Canadian things so I was determined to make movies as un-Canadian as possible.'[49] In part because of this overt hostility, 'Maddin's films have been poor fodder for a criticism which seeks to trace links between characteristics of works and the condition of life in English Canada'[50] However, when considering the films themselves as a body of work, we are confronted by another impasse. In the first review of his work *The Dead Father*, the writer assumed Maddin's setting, the 'Dominion of Forgetfulness,' was the 'Dominion of Canada.' *Tales from the Gimli Hospital* was explicitly identified with regional specificity. *Archangel* featured a Canadian soldier as a hero. *The Saddest Music in the World* was set in Winnipeg. Even the Tolzbadians of *Careful* behaved in what Maddin calls 'a Canuck manner.'[51] Rather than trying to resolve this issue one way or another, it might be more useful to think about the manner in which critics interpret Maddin's work as an ideological marker. The project of constructing a 'national' film canon itself is arguably a fantasy that occludes the very problems that criticism should be attempting to address.

Perhaps these structural ambiguities are part of what makes *My Winnipeg* attractive to a range of audiences, because the film has garnered a great deal of favourable attention. *My Winnipeg* won the Best Canadian Feature award at the Toronto International Film Festival in 2006. In his wrap piece for *Variety* on that year's festival, Todd McCarthy wrote, 'I've been coming to the Toronto film festival for more than twenty years, and I can safely say that this is the first time I've been able to make the following statement: the two best new films I saw here this year were by Canadian directors. The men responsible for this unusual state of affairs were David Cronenberg and Guy Maddin.'[52] *My Winnipeg* was also awarded the Toronto Film Critics Association's Rogers Best Canadian Film Award for 2008, a relatively new award with a $10,000 prize attached. In addition, it appeared on 2008 year-end top ten lists from critics at the *Austin Chronicle* (both Marjorie Baumgarten and Mark Savlov), the *Globe and Mail* (both Liam Lacey and Rick Groen), *The Village Voice* (Jim Hoberman), *The Onion AV Club* (Noel Murray), *TIME Magazine* (Richard Corliss), and many others.[53] On 30 December 2009 Roger Ebert

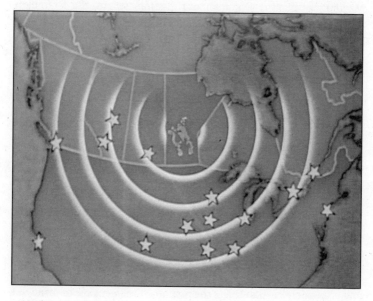

The heart of the continent. Courtesy of Guy Maddin, from the director's personal collection.

named *My Winnipeg* as one of the top ten films of the first decade of the twenty-first century.[53]

The general critical consensus on *My Winnipeg* is that it sits at or very near the apex of Maddin's oeuvre. Denis Seguin writes, 'Maddin's genius lies in his balance. He performs a complicated tightrope act, treading the line between homage and mockery, nostalgia and kitsch, drama and camp. And he keeps the audience off balance while we watch, waiting for him to fall and for us to fall with him. *My Winnipeg* may be his greatest balancing act of all, particularly when the narration is delivered live from the stage.'[55] Joe Morgenstern sees *My Winnipeg* as a breakthrough film that moves beyond formalist pastiche: 'this autobiographical meditation is seductively funny, as well as deliciously strange, and hauntingly beautiful, as well as stream-of-consciousness cockeyed. And the film succeeds partly thanks to, rather than in spite of, its swirling, mostly black-and-white images that might have been downloaded from a fevered dream.'[56] Jim Hoberman called it 'Maddin's best filmmaking since the not-dissimilar confessional bargain-basement phantasmagoria, *Cowards Bend the Knee*.'[57] Philip Kennicott mentions 'the masterly manipulation of tone that makes Maddin's work so compelling, entertaining and powerful.'[58] Though critics have been divided on the merits of many of Maddin's past works, it is actually quite difficult to find a thoroughly negative review of *My Winnipeg*.

One final thing is also worth keeping in mind in terms of critical responses to this film, particularly in those that find something lacking (what we might call the *My* Winnipeg vs. *My Winnipeg* Problem). As Nezar AlSayyad points out, when Walter Ruttmann's film *Berlin: die Sinfonie einer Grossstadt/Berlin: Symphony of a Great City* – a film that was influential in the conceptual stages of *My Winnipeg* – appeared in 1927, 'various contemporaries recognized enough of "their" Berlin in Ruttmann's film to decry the absence of those other parts that "should" have been included. But here, critiques of *Berlin* also serve our attempts to understand industrial modernity.' Ruttmann's film's debut coincided with 'an intense debate on the ethical values of urban life in Weimar Germany'[59] that is in many respects similar to the ferment of discussion taking place about the nature of cities and city life today. It would serve us well to consider the kinds of responses to Maddin's film in terms of the discourse around urbanity in our own era.

# The Peculiar Enchantments of Winnipeg: The Commission

Don't please give us the frozen hellhole we know it is.
                                        – Michael Burns to Guy Maddin[1]

Maddin has remarked that he finds it easiest to dig into a new film-making project when someone has given him a task,[2] and *My Winnipeg* falls into this category. The taskmaster in question was Michael Burns, the commissioning editor of the Documentary Channel at the time, who asked Maddin if he'd ever considered making a full-length documentary. Burns had previously produced *My Dad Is 100 Years Old* (2005), a short film directed by Maddin but written and performed by Isabella Rossellini as a tribute to her father, Roberto Rossellini (available as a DVD tipped into Rossellini's book *In the Name of the Father, the Daughter and the Holy Spirits*).[3] Maddin initially found the idea too daunting for a variety of reasons; documentaries generally require a fair amount of research and preparation, they have a very high ratio of filming to the actual amount of usable footage, and they allow for a daunting amount of freedom in the editing process. However, penury is a great motivator. When Maddin was running low on money, he called Burns to see if he was still interested in some sort of commission.[4]

Burns had two suggestions for Maddin: a film about the trains of Winnipeg (inspired, Maddin believes, by Burns's trip through Winni-

The Frozen Forks: a preparatory storyboard collage. Courtesy of Guy
Maddin, from the director's personal collection.

peg in the late 1970s escorting a steam train to Alberta for use on the set of Terrence Malick's *Days of Heaven*), or a film about Winnipeg itself. Burns's only other trip to Winnipeg that Maddin knew of was to visit the director on the set of *My Dad Is 100 Years Old*.[5] What happened on that set, Maddin believes, irrevocably skewed Burns's sense of Winnipeg towards the mythic: 'Isabella Rossellini emerged out of the darkness like in a David Lynch moment, and whispered a few warm, moist, Scanda-Italian syllables into his ear ... so he really wanted to see some sort of film that conveyed the peculiar enchantments of Winnipeg.'[6] Burns thus gave Maddin carte blanche to present an utterly subjective, personal take on the city. His closing plea to Maddin, as the director recounts in the official 'Soda Pictures Theatrical Press Kit,' was 'don't please give us the frozen hellhole we know it is.'

The first outline for the film emerged the day after Maddin called Burns. Maddin was in Paris screening *The Saddest Music in the World* at the Pompidou Centre when an audience member asked him to describe Winnipeg. The director spent ten or fifteen minutes outlining his thoughts and feelings about his home, which he says he'd never really done before. Nevertheless, in that one précis, he covered most of the subjects that actually appeared in the film. Afterwards, he returned to his hotel room and wrote an email to Burns summarizing this material.[7]

Nevertheless, *My Winnipeg* didn't emerge from Maddin's head fully formed. His first inclination was to attempt a pastiche of Fellini's *I Vitelloni*. 'I wanted to not just have myself wandering around town, but four of my dearest friends from my twenty-something most useless years. Just these kind of guys wandering around like lazy drones, experiencing the city and visiting things.'[8] ('The drones' is the epithet that Maddin's amorphous crew of long-time male friends have always used to describe themselves.) However, the first draft of the film was rejected, and Maddin himself soon came to the conclusion that Barry Levinson's *Diner* (1982) had already covered the *I Vitteloni* remake territory sufficiently that such an approach would require too large a cast and, in any event, didn't *feel* much like a documentary to him.[10] Though the drones disappeared as the subject matter of the film, Maddin's friends continued to exert influence behind the camera, providing him with a constant stream of local folklore, rumours, half-truths, and anecdotes to transform into subject matter.

What remained after banishing the aimless, aging dandies of his early adulthood from the centre of the narrative was their wandering itself. Walking became both the process that helped Maddin to generate new ideas for the film and eventually one of *My Winnipeg*'s thematic concerns and the basis for its formal structure. 'There's something about walking that's better than driving, better than sitting in front of a word processor, even, for digging up ideas,' Maddin tells Michael Ondaatje.[11] While walking his then girlfriend's pug, Spanky, four times a day over the winter months, often in the company of filmmaker Noam Gonick, Maddin ruminated over various ideas for the form that *My Winnipeg* might eventually take. Despite the current vogue for Symbolist *flânerie* and Situationist psychogeography, Maddin's touchstones were, as usual, just far enough off the cultural radar to give his work a unique inflection. One influence was Oskar Fischinger's 1927 short film, *Walking from Munich to Berlin*, in which Fischinger made a series of 1-second shots with his camera as he strolled between the two cities. As a tribute to both Fischinger's film and the now deceased Spanky, Maddin made a 4-minute filmic record of one winter walk at his cabin in Gimli titled *Spanky – To the Pier and Back* (2008), which appears on the DVD of *My Winnipeg*.

Maddin was also influenced by the walking literature of Jean-Jacques Rousseau, Robert Walser, and, especially, W.G. Sebald. 'I guess I was really emboldened by the writing of W.G. Sebald who just goes on these walks and then goes into little reminiscing digressions and things like that,' says Maddin. 'I certainly wouldn't flatter myself that I'm Sebaldian, but I abandoned *I Vitelloni* and decided to think Sebald.'[12] Despite

Maddin's demurral, there are strong similarities between the structure of Sebald's prose and *My Winnipeg*. Massimo Leone portrays Sebald's prose as a mixture of 'fictional stories imbued with autobiographical fragments, essays whose verisimilitude is mixed with far-fetched details, realistic travelogues peppered with dreams and hallucinations, intertextual references or pseudo-references, words that caption images and images that illustrate words' – a set of descriptors that could easily apply to *My Winnipeg*, as could his observation about the structure of Sebald's work. Despite beginning with this textual hodgepodge, Sebald 'is so skilful in erasing his own organising function that his continuous and systematic digressions flow in an apparently steady stream, the voice of the narrator discreetly intervening only to guide the reader from one micro-narrative to the next.'[13]

Walking is a direct solution to one of the problems that Maddin faced when attempting to make a film about Winnipeg. Throughout his interviews and essays, Maddin repeats the same refrain about the 'inability of Winnipeggers to mythologize, or even remember, their history';[14] throughout his films, Winnipeg is always a city of amnesiacs and sleepwalkers. As Michel de Certeau notes, local legends are one of the ways that city dwellers make the urban landscape liveable, because they provide imaginary entrances and exits, turning dead ends into dwelling places, literally making a place accessible. In the case of a place that lacks legends, or can't or won't remember the ones it once had, travel in general and walking in particular produces 'precisely the body of legends that is currently lacking in one's own vicinity' by creating a passage to something other than the mundane. In this respect, walking and dreaming – one of Maddin's other metaphors for creating Winnipeg's elsewhere – have the same structure. Both produce new legends through a series of displacements of things from one place and condensing them in another[15] If 'Winnipeg is an oubliette,'[16] travelling in and out of it and walking around it transforms it into a home.

Once Maddin had some working notes for a treatment, he began to construct a screenplay by recording improvisations, because the idea of sitting down and writing eighty minutes of script seemed too daunting. His producers, Michael Burns at the Documentary Channel and his regular producer, Jody Shapiro, were united on the subject that Maddin should narrate the film in his own voice,[17] for the reason that 'there were so many implausible myths in the movie that if I'd hired a narrator to be me that would just push it over into pure fiction.'[18] Maddin began the process by working with his long-time friend, the journalist Robert Enright, who conducted a series of interviews with the director with the intention of bringing some interesting material to light. Despite Maddin's belief that Enright has always been the best at drawing him out in conversation, he felt that there was no spontaneity to the material that this process generated, and in the end he used only a few lines of it. After pondering what other processes for generating text remained, Maddin recalled his experience on S*U*R*V*I*V*A*L during a three-month period when Greg Klymkiw went into hiding after a violent altercation with his father after the latter discovered his role on the show. The premise that was decided on to explain Klymkiw's absence from the set was that Trevor Winthrop-Baines had been kidnapped. It was Maddin's job to write the ransom notes, and then, in character as Concerned Citizen Stan, he read them back to the television audience on the set of the show. Because he had enjoyed this process, Maddin decided to revive something similar for *My Winnipeg.*

He began an extensive series of sessions with sound engineer Michel Germain, in which he would prepare and then read back 'stylish little things – it wasn't just improvised off the top of my head.' Over a period of about six weeks, for five minutes a day at 5 p.m., with these notes as a starting point, Maddin attempted to produce a sufficient flow of verbiage about the city to generate the film's narration.[19] When he ran out of things to say, he began to repeat himself until he conceived of something new. Maddin contends that this is the source of the trip-licate repetitions in the narrative, but such repetitions are already a characteristic feature of the intertitles in several of his earlier films. Out of the lassitude that this process induced in Germain, Maddin was inspired to return to the subject of hypnosis once again, but this time not focusing on his actors: 'I realized I possessed the power of a Mesmer, Reveen, Romane or any of the immortal stage hypnotists and their ilk, and that rather than squandering this eerie power pulling the bras off beautiful women – oh, the ephemeral vanity of that gesture! – I would use it in the service of cinema … to hypnotize my entire audience.'[20] This narration also literally became the rhythm of the editing of the film; Maddin first had Germain cut the narration 'like a radio show' and then had John Gurdebecke cut the film's footage to the narration in the way that he would normally use music to set a tempo.[21]

Though music had played a significant role in both the editing and the final presentation of several of Maddin's recent films (*Dracula: Pages from a Virgin's Diary*, where the score works hand-in-hand with the choreography; *The Saddest Music in the World*, a musical; and *Brand Upon the Brain!*, which toured with a live orchestra), in *My Winnipeg* it takes a back seat to the narration. The music in *My Winnipeg* comes from a variety of sources: public domain tracks from various Poverty Row films, snatches of classical music – Prokofiev, Wagner from *Tristan und Isolde* – and compositions by Jason Staczek, who had written the music for *Brand Upon the Brain!*. Whereas the music Staczek wrote for *Brand* was scored for a full orchestra, the tracks included in *My Winnipeg* were all MIDI.[22]

Unlike the narration, all of the dialogue for *My Winnipeg* was written by George Toles, which is standard practice for Maddin's films. 'I just like the way [Toles] manners human speech,' says Maddin. 'He insists that all of his characters speak in complete sentences and with proper punctuation. It makes naturalism a tough achievement for an actor.'[23] What makes this situation seem somewhat odd is that all of the dialogue in the film concerns Maddin's childhood reminiscences of intimate family conversations. This literal element of uncanniness – a rendering of the homely (*heimlich*) as unhomely (*unheimlich*) – is perfectly in keeping with the tone that pervades the city symphony as a genre in general and *My Winnipeg* in particular. What makes this film stick in the memory is the nagging suspicion that this weird quality haunting the very heart of the everyday is not some sort of exception particular to Maddin's family (either the historical individuals or their various onscreen doppelgängers), but the rule (for Winnipeg? for Canada? for everyone?) itself.

Because the real star of *My Winnipeg* is the city, casting was not a long or complicated procedure. Many of the smaller roles in the film were played by Maddin regulars, notably the following. Louis Negin (Mayor Cornish) wrote the narration for *Brand Upon the Brain!* and appeared as Dr. Fusi in *Cowards Bend the Knee* and as the Blind Seer in *The Saddest Music in the World* as well as in larger roles in Maddin's short films *Sissy Boy Slap Party* (2004) and *Glorious* (2008). Amy Stewart (Janet Maddin) was also Veronica in *Cowards Bend the Knee*. Stewart, who has been an actor since childhood, is also the niece of Maddin's brother Cameron's girlfriend, Carol Isaac. After Carol's untimely death during Maddin's childhood, the teenage Cameron took his own life at her graveside. For Maddin, Carol's family has always been a species of in-law. Casting Carol as a ghost in *Cowards*, Maddin tells Robert Enright, 'made me feel quite mischevious;'[24] casting her as his sister likely evokes a similar feeling, but Maddin was impressed enough with her previous work that he was confident that 'she could simply direct herself while I wrestled with Ann Savage, who hadn't heard a slate crack in fifty years.' Both Kate Yacula (Citizen Girl) and Jacelyn Lobay (Gwenyth Lloyd) appeared in *Odin's Shield Maiden* (2006). Darcy Fehr, who played 'Guy Maddin' in *Cowards Bend the Knee*, reappears as Ledgeman and as the sleeping figure on the train at the opening of the film. The focus

Guy Maddin (foreground) and Darcy Fehr (background). Courtesy of
Guy Maddin, from the director's personal collection.

on Fehr in this shot, coupled with Maddin's first-person narration ('If only I can stay awake,' and so on) strongly suggests that the figure on the train is another 'Guy Maddin' avatar. 'I see Darcy's credited himself as me on IMDb,' chuckles Maddin, adding to the ambiguity.[25] Brendan and Wesley Cade, who play Cameron and Ross Maddin, were located for Maddin by a casting agent. Fred Dunsmore, the legendary centre who led the Winnipeg Maroons to the Allan Cup in 1964, plays himself, as does Lou Profeta, alleged local exorcist of furniture, streetcars, and other inanimate objects.

Which leaves the role of Mother. 'A force as strong as all the trains in Manitoba. As perennial as winter. As ancient as the bison. As supernatural as the forks themselves,' intones the narration. In his annotations to the script of *My Winnipeg*, Maddin writes, 'I knew there was only one person alive, who had *ever* lived, who could play the role of my mother.'[26] That person was Ann Savage.

Before her role in *My Winnipeg*, Ann Savage (1921–2008) was primarily known for one incandescent performance, as Vera in Edgar G. Ulmer's Poverty Row film noir classic, *Detour* (1945). In Savage's obituary in the *Village Voice*, Roy Edroso described *Detour* as perhaps 'the most hopeless and deterministic *noir* picture ever,'[27] a reputation largely due to Savage's performance. Since Savage's death, the eulogy on the *Please Pass the Popcorn* blog has become the definitive description of this role: '"Femme fatale" doesn't even come close to describing what Savage does in this movie. Savage's character would eat a femme fatale for breakfast. And then beat another femme fatale to death with the first one's bones.'[28] Savage's film career began in 1938, when she appeared as an extra in *The Great Waltz*. Throughout the 1940s she made a number of B movies, including four with Tom Neal, her co-star in *Detour*. After a 1944 photo shoot in *Esquire*, Savage also became a favourite pin-up for the troops during World War II. By the early 1950s, Savage's main appearances were in guest star roles on television serials, and by the mid-1950s, she had effectively retired, appearing in only a few minor roles over the next five decades (including an episode of *Saved by the Bell*).

Eddie Muller, the author of several crime novels and critical books on film noir and a friend of Maddin, introduced him to Savage. A complex process of wooing began, with extensive phone calls; Maddin made trips to Hollywood and eventually offered part of his own salary ($10,000 U.S. out of his $50,000 Canadian, plus the initial $1,200 she had been offered) and a three-picture deal to Savage before she was convinced to take the role. On subsequent trips to meet with her in Hollywood, Maddin says that she would occasionally put a few thousand dollars in an envelope and slip it to him, so he ended up getting half of the money back. Savage insisted to Maddin from the outset (in full noir femme-fatale idiom) that she had never retired: 'This talk of being away from film doesn't cut any ice with me!' Kent Adamson, her guardian, confirmed that every morning at 4 a.m., Savage would do her make-up, put on her furs, and go out to do character studies in preparation for future roles. By the time she arrived on set, Maddin says, she was 'spitting tacks.' Though the film begins with Maddin prompting Savage with her lines, the director graciously says, 'I do that for everybody.'[29] Maddin views her presence in the film as a direct injection of old-school Hollywood aura into the production: 'her face … seized the camera, arrested it and literally loaded up even the cheapest new film-stick emulsions with quantities of silver not used in Hollywood since the forties.'[30] In the hands of a director who clearly adored her performances past and present, what could easily have become an exercise in exploitative kitsch became, instead, a sharp, funny performance that serves as a dignified coda to Savage's career.

Crewing *My Winnipeg* was 'a bad experience,' Maddin says. 'I heard a lot of crew members complaining that the pay was bad. I still don't know how little everyone made, but I know the producer and the line producer say it wasn't that bad.' With two U.S. films shooting in the city simultaneously and providing competitive employment opportunities, Maddin had crew members quitting two days into the ten-day shoot and seeking work elsewhere. Before the first day of shooting, the production had gone through five DOPs (directors of photography) alone. As a result, Maddin's producer, Jody Shapiro, also took on the role of DOP. Shapiro did the majority of the filming, and Maddin did subsequent pick-up shots, such as the train sequence. Evan Johnson, Maddin's intern, was commissioned to do a lot of footage of signage, and various visitors to the set were, as is customary on a Maddin shoot, sometimes simply handed a camera and told to begin filming.[31]

The great majority of Maddin's films over the years have been shot on 16mm black and white stock, with some subsequent tinting (the major exceptions are *Careful*, shot in a mix of 16mm black and white and something resembling two-strip Technicolor, and *Twilight of the Ice Nymphs*, shot in 35mm colour). Production techniques on *My Winnipeg*, on the other hand, began simply but became increasingly complex. Maddin says, 'I had originally shot a lot more of it in video and color because I really wanted to use this movie to help me break through to the digital realm. But I finally decided, just at the last minute, to project a lot of the video sequences that had been edited and re-photograph them on film, just to embed them in emulsion instead. Just consign them to the world of memory and lament.'[32] As a result, the media employed in the production of *My Winnipeg* include Super-8, 16mm, mini-DV, HD video, conventional video, stock footage, home movies, animation shot on video, and animation shot on Super-8. Finally, Maddin found some sections of the digital video to be too sharp, so in order to add texture, he projected them onto his fridge and refilmed them.[33]

Maddin's signature visual aesthetic evokes, but does not replicate, the look that films made in the 1920s might have after decades of projection, splicing, scratching, duplication, discoloration, and general wear and tear. This look comes from a complex brew of digital and analog recording and editing techniques, augmented with an unabashedly primitivist approach towards conventional filmic values like continuity. Maddin says, 'I have gotten most of my atmospheric effects through screw-ups on my camera,' but then laments that 'these new HD cameras are kind of screw-up proof.'[34] Hybrid processes like reshooting projected digital footage on film, on the other hand, can produce satisfactorily 'weird digital artifacts and weird bars and flickers,' which he often ends up pleading with his editor to retain. Some of the filming on *My Winnipeg* also involved re-enactments, mixing rear-projected archival footage, still photos, animation and live actors. Maddin imagines this kitchen-sink approach as tonally perfect for depicting Winnipeg on film, because it 'has always been a rags and bones kind of city. Lots of old country people, or their ghosts still wandering round peddling off their rag carts – the junk man and his horse drawn cart going down back lanes. One second he's there, one second he's gone – never too sure what going on and the city is really a blizzard of tattered narrative fragments blowing around from past, present and possibly the future.'[35]

One of the factors that propelled this technical farrago was the inclusion in *My Winnipeg* of stock footage. Maddin says, 'I'd never used stock footage in a movie before. I took a point of pride in that.' He adds that worrying about its appearance in contrast to footage that he and his crew had shot was part of what prompted him to include so many other different looks and textures. There is actually surprisingly little stock footage to be seen in *My Winnipeg*. Maddin speculates that 'not many Winnipegers had movie cameras, or if they did, their films have either been lost forever or haven't made their way into the archives.'[36] The majority of stock footage in the film comes from only a handful of sources: some track images from a documentary about a train trip to Hudson Bay; Fox newsreel footage of If Day; the Holly Snowshoe Club's footage; and the Maddin family's home movies.

If Day was a massive 5,000-person enactment of a Nazi invasion in Winnipeg that took place on 14 February 1942, as part of a federal government campaign to raise Victory bonds to fund the national war effort. The *Winnipeg Tribune* estimated that 40 million people at the time knew about If Day, because nearly every major North American daily paper and all newsreel corporations covered the event.[37] Nevertheless, the event has faded out of the memories of all but a few historians and those willing to pore over the minutiae of forgotten texts. Maddin learned of If Day only because he loaned a copy of *Winnipeg 100*, a coffee-table book commemorating the city's 1973 centenary, to Andy Smetanka, the filmmaker who contributed the animated sequences to *My Winnipeg*, for source material, and Smetanka drew the event to his attention.'[38] the only footage of If Day that Maddin was able to locate was in the possession of Fox Newsreels and cost an exorbitant amount, so he purchased only a few seconds of it.'[39] According to the annotated script, the majority of archival footage in the firm comes from twenty minutes of 16mm movies shot by the members of the Holly Snowshoe Club before its thirty-fifth anniversary in 1935.[40]

Some of the Maddin family's 8mm home movies that appear in the film were shot by the director himself, and some were shot by Maddin's older brother, Ross, before Guy was two years old, 'this eerily dark pre-adolescent cinematography earning him, a half-century later, an "additional camera" credit in the tail roll of *My Winnipeg*.'[41] These home movies provide an opportunity to reflect on the function that the inclusion of found footage has in any film. Documentary film critic Bill Nichols has observed that home movies function very differently depending on who is actually watching them. For family and friends, such footage has 'clear documentary value,' but for everyone else, it works radically differently, serving as a more generic document of the kinds of events that people might have decided were worth filming, and of the ways that people presented themselves before a camera in a given culture at a particular historical moment. In other words, 'one person's historical evidence is another person's fiction.' Both fiction film and documentary make use of the same strategies for establishing referentiality. Even a specific identifiable person (Guy Maddin) may be a historical person in one shot and an actor in another.[42] The salient point is, as critic Stella Bruzzi argues, that any use of archival material in the construction of a larger work such as a non-fiction film is necessarily artificial and subjective. Even though historical documents show us one aspect of an event that we normally assume to be definitively over and therefore static, the past is 'infinitely accessible through interpretation and recontextualization, and thus becomes a mutable, not a constant, point of reference.'[43] Maddin's unabashed subjectivity in *My Winnipeg* lays bare what is ultimately true of all film, let alone all documentary. Which raises another question: exactly what sort of film is *My Winnipeg* anyway?

# A Glorious Dress-up Chest: Genre

I wasn't literally trying to go through film history, but I did sort of want to touch on as many outré genres, genres that had fallen out of fashion, as possible.

– Guy Maddin to William Beard[1]

When mulling over the relationship that Guy Maddin's films bear to existing genres, one of the most common strategies critics use is to treat them as *sui generis*. Phrases such as 'a genre that Maddin invented himself, a genre that is at once beyond definition, and yet all too familiar to those already familiar with the director's past works' characterize many of the responses to Maddin's early and mid-career films.[2] Some versions of the posters and other promotional materials created for *My Winnipeg*, which bear the subtitle 'A Docu-fantasia by Guy Maddin,' seem to assent to this notion by coining an entirely new portmanteau word to describe it. Since the film's completion, however, Maddin himself has expressed some doubts about the value of this gesture. '[Docu-fantasia] was a term we've applied because we thought some people would balk with us telling them that it was a documentary, but I think I'm backing off of that term. I think it is just a documentary. Documentary has elastic enough borders, especially now, everyone understands that there is no such thing as a completely honest documentary. Everything has a point of view.'[3]

One useful way to characterize Maddin's treatment of genre in his films is as *dialogic* in the sense that Mikhail Bakhtin used the term. One genre rarely comes to dominate in any given Maddin film, but several identifiable genres often coexist in a kind of perpetual, roiling conversation, in which various tendencies gain ascendancy at one point and then fade into the background at others. Because no single point of view tends to dominate for long, there is no place inside such a film for an objective, non-participating perspective on the part of Maddin's narrators, which makes it difficult for a viewer to comfortably reduce the whole to some sort of conventional category.[4]

This is not to say that Maddin is uninterested in the question of genre, because, if anything, the opposite is true. Maddin tells Zachary Wigon: 'I really groped in the editing process for a form. I thought I could cheat the whole documentary-making process by just making shot lists and pretending the thing was one big fiction, and just shooting it like a narrative film. But you can't cheat documentary, so I had to go back and shoot even more stuff that, as the editing evolved, demanded gaps to be filled.'[5] What the notion of dialogism provides is a way of addressing the constant push and pull between the dictates of specific historical forms and an individual director's innovations. Maddin and Ondaatje address this dialogic tug-of-war directly in their conversation:

MO: Well, something happens, I think, when you are obsessed with something and then you are shaping it as something out there. You're objectifying it and then the form takes over and deals with it in a more objective way.

GM: Yes, no matter how honest and true you're trying to be about yourself, you're still dealing with a third person somehow, that's shaping that Guy Maddin or that work. I'm sure that must happen with you all the time.

MO: It's strange because you're so intensely involved with the thing and then the form can come in and govern the story ...

GM: You're not Michael or Guy anymore – you're a reader or viewer and
you just have to worry about the forms.[6]

At the precise moments when we are trying to express the 'honest and
true' specificities of our lives, the vast, impersonal dictates of form and
genre reassert themselves, making supposedly unique individuals con-
form to some sort of larger pattern. This phenomenon appears elsewhere in Maddin's work on a smaller scale, in the director's willing-
ness to cede the scripting of his childhood memories to George Toles's
highly formal prose, but it also holds true at the level of the film itself.
In the words of Matt Zoller Seitz, Maddin's focus on genres rather than
historical periods transforms cinema history into 'a kind of glorious
dress-up chest.'[7]

A spectrum of genres reside in the musty depths of the *My Winnipeg* Tickle Trunk. At one extreme is the documentary, and at the other,
melodrama, which William Beard argues characterizes Maddin's entire
oeuvre.[8] These two broad and disparate tendencies manifest themselves in yet another 1920s sub-genre, the city symphony or 'cross-
section,' which is roomy enough to include both. After a few general
comments on documentary and melodrama, I will look more closely at
the city symphony genre and its relationship to *My Winnipeg*.

As Maddin has observed on several occasions, the notion of what
constitutes a documentary is more accommodating than it used to be.
Bill Nichols explains: 'Traditionally, the word *documentary* has suggested
fullness and completion, knowledge and fact, explanations of the social
world and its motivating mechanisms. More recently, though, documentary has come to suggest incompleteness and uncertainty, recol-
lection and impression, images of personal worlds and their subjective
constitution.'[9] For Stella Bruzzi, the documentary form itself is inher-
ently dialogic, 'a perpetual negotiation between the real event and its
representation,' where the two remain distinct from each other but

Ledgeman: family romance as daily dose of melodrama. Courtesy of Guy Maddin, from the director's personal collection.

interact constantly. A documentary is always occupying a space on a continuum with the idea of the film (particularly archival footage) as an objective historical record at one end, connoting an ideal of representational purity, and narration on the other end, because it always adds a subjective interpretation to the events that are unfolding onscreen.[10]

One of the other ways in which all documentaries demonstrate their particular biases is in terms of which material they choose to depict and which is excluded because it either was never filmed or ended up on the (increasingly metaphorical) cutting-room floor. Making a documentary necessarily involves subjective selections merely because one film cannot depict every aspect of a given topic. At 80 minutes in length, *My Winnipeg* is already shorter than many features, but not because of a lack of material. Maddin jokes 'There was much more to say. I literally could have done *Winnipeg Alexanderplatz* with this, but I didn't want to try everyone's patience.'[11] When audiences complain about what is 'missing' from Maddin's film, what becomes obvious is that, like found footage, any city can be infinitely recontextualized and re-presented. Wolfgang Natter adds that in any documentary about a city, the place that has been captured on film no longer exists by the time the film is released, so there is never an 'original' with which to compare the film for verisimilitude. What documentaries about cities do, then, is turn physical spaces into necessarily fragmented, partial 'places of memory.'[12]

Given Maddin's avowed fondness for working from small, well-crafted fragments of text, it is relatively predictable that, throughout his interviews and published essays, set pieces that Maddin has constructed tend to appear in almost identical form in multiple locations. One of these set pieces is Maddin's definition of melodrama. Maddin credits renowned theatre critic and Brecht expert Eric Bentley as the original source of this notion, but his own version has become well polished over the years, as he says he almost always ends up talking about melodrama in interviews. This is the version he presented to me, which is similar to the one that he presents in the documentary *97 Percent True* and in other interviews, but it contains more detail. Accordingly, I repeat it here at length, because it constitutes a major statement of Maddin's aesthetic:

In waking life, we are continually compelled to restrain ourselves. You're not really allowed to weep openly when you're sad; when you're angry you're discouraged from yelling at them, and you're constrained by law from hitting a person you hate; if you see someone you lust after, you're not just allowed to grab them and have your way. All sorts of everyday impulses are constantly repressed by rules of decorum and the law.

But in your dreams, if you're lucky, you get to grab anyone after whom you lust. You get to cry and wail; you get to express loudly your terror of things without feeling any embarrassment. You're basically living all of your feelings in an uninhibited state. This is part of Bentley's definition too: dreaming adults and children and neurotics all get to be uninhibited without surprising anybody or being improper.

What this sets up is the concept of uninhibition instead of exaggeration. A lot of people think melodrama is the truth exaggerated, but he says it's the truth uninhibited. There's a big difference: if you take something that's true and exaggerate it, you are distorting it, and it may no longer be true. If you take the truth, which is barely discernible, and uninhibit it, you're actually making it more visible, and there's no distortion at all. You're just bringing it out to the surface in a good melodrama.

I try to point out to students of melodrama that when they see something implausible, they should see it as an uninhibition. When a long story is told in a melodramatic style, it can be fit in to a short period of time because you can uninhibit things. You can have a jealous person showing their jealousy in ways that advance the plot in a hurry. You can have them poisoning someone or murdering someone, but those actions are just standing in for jealousy. You don't really need to see if they jive with your model of the human heart because you don't really need to see them as literal murders ... So once you start viewing movies not as grotesque and tasteless exaggerations but as sincere and honest manifestations of real and plausible psychological dynamics, you can tell a good melodrama from a bad one.[13]

In some important respects, this statement differs significantly from the theorization that William Beard presents in 'Maddin and Melodrama.' Beard argues that 'the glaring excess of Maddin's melodrama is then a deliberate exaggeration, an exaggeration unto parody, of perceptions and affects that cannot be expressed in a more uncovered form in the contemporary environment.' The difference between the two accounts has to do with divergent implicit assumptions about the nature of contemporary culture, and with divergent assumptions about what exactly is being manifested in the melodramatic moments in Maddin's films. Beard sees Maddin's melodramatic excess as the symptom of the return of repressed 'naïve and extreme emotions, rooted in childhood and requiring a quasi-childlike intensity and directness of expression' under prohibitive 'adult' cultural conditions that render them grotesque in appearance. As such, he argues, it is our culture that is sick, not Maddin's films, because it has no room for the 'proper' expression of such emotion.[14]

What is missing from Beard's analysis is the recognition that the overall rules of culture have changed. As a result, Maddin's films do not function culturally in the way that Beard describes them as functioning. Far from repressing naïve and extreme emotions under a stern edict to conduct ourselves with decorum, contemporary culture urges us to revel in such emotions and to indulge in all possible forms of excessive behaviour, precisely in order to render them ineffectual. Slavoj Žižek has written extensively about this 'shift in perspective,' arguing that what in modern culture appeared as subversive and marginal has, in postmodernity, moved to culture's very core.[15] Evidence of this shift is everywhere, but we need look no further than the fact that Maddin's taboo-breaking films, which Beard cheerfully describes as 'a carnival of amputation, corpse-violation and other instances of corporeal abjection,'[16] routinely receive funding from a variety of quite respectable governmental cultural agencies, then go on to win major awards. Their content is actually the *least* scandalous aspect of these films. Beard's reading, which proceeds according to a classically modernist 'symptomal' analysis, positions Maddin's texts as subversive, marginal manifestations of a hidden truth that official culture had to repress in order to establish itself at a time when official culture represses almost nothing.[17] As such, it misses its mark.

The truth that emerges in Maddin's films is a different sort of entity altogether. In postmodern culture, truth appears not in marginal, symbolic practices that subvert a restrictive social order, but in effects of the Real – of traumatic moments that resist symbolization altogether.[18] There are a number of ways to conceive of such moments in Maddin's films. One approach might be to focus in detail on the material qualities that these films flaunt – grainy or high-contrast film, visual noise, digital glitches, abrupt switches between media types, and continuity gaps; or the soundtrack's hisses, pops, tinny tones, acousmatic voices, and scratches. In the particular case of *My Winnipeg*, though, another aspect of the truth lies in the irresolvable tension created by the gap between documentary and melodrama. As Žižek argues, what first appears as a question of form ('how, in what order, to tell the story') is 'symptomatic of a more radical deadlock that pertains to the social content itself'; it tells us something 'about a certain gap that is *stricto sensu* a fundamental *social fact*.'[19] That gap concerns not just the way we film cities, but the way that we imagine them with the help of film. This gap is as old as the relationship between films and cities, which, as we shall see, means that it defines an impasse that is one of the constitutive elements of modernity itself.

Along with the distance between the spectator and spectacle, the difference between the everyday and the fantastic also crumbles. *My Winnipeg* presents a cityscape where historical truths can appear bizarre and fantasies seem utterly mundane. Everything is levelled under a blanket of snow and dream. Snow, drugs, sleep, and sex all serve as narcotic forces that create a screen ready for the projection of the contents of the director's imagination. At least for a while. One of the marks of the success of *My Winnipeg* as a work of art is that all of its fantasies ultimately *fail*.

The narrative of his birth and early childhood that Maddin presents in the annotated script of *My Winnipeg* is based entirely around a fantasy relation to the screen. In this little set piece, young Guy's recognition of the TV as a fellow creature or mirror image is purely, onanistically Imaginary, interrupted only by the prohibitive presence of his sister: 'both of us growing in each other's cathode gaze … It wasn't till my sister noticed one of us masturbating in front of the unblinking stare of the other that our perhaps too-close relationship was called into question.'[20] The point is not that Maddin identifies with the TV ('one of us' is masturbating) to the extent that he has eroticized the relationship and that his sister is ruining his fun, but that he actually identifies with the perspective of his sister. By presenting this situation in a fantasy scenario, as is the case whenever some version of 'Guy Maddin' is on the screen, Maddin is writing satire, ridiculing his own weaknesses and shortcomings from a perspective removed from and critical of his on-screen double.[21]

The reconstruction of Maddin's childhood home at 800 Ellice has a similar kind ambivalence and does interesting things to our notion of 'documentary.' Replacing historical reality with fantastic objects, such as Maddin's substituting a family of actors for his real family, erases or destroys realistic referentiality, but at the same time makes it possible to realize the director's inner world. As Stella Bruzzi comments in the 2006 edition of her book *New Documentary*, since the turn of the millennium, when the first edition of the book was published, there was a noticeable rise in 'dramatic reconstruction as a supplement or even replacement for archival material.' As is consistently the case in his films, Maddin brings about this moment of innovation (which, the narration claims, could actually 'create a whole new genre of film') by a return to 1920s forms. Bruzzi observes that in documentaries made in the 1920s in the U.S.S.R., reconstruction was used interchangeably with archival footage.[22] What has changed, of course, is that the explicit claim to revolutionary political meaning has dropped away from the form. Something to ponder, though, is whether Maddin's allegedly inept documenting of the broken aftermath of the great urban project of modernity does not still contain some critical force.

The rationale that directors like Oliver Stone present for the use of reconstruction in contemporary documentaries is usually quite earnest. Stone hopes that it might be 'possible to intervene in the process by which truth is constructed.'[23] Maddin's version of historical reconstruction in *My Winnipeg*, on the other hand, seems doomed from the outset because of its shoddiness. In fact, the end product Maddin seems to be after as a director is to produce one of the 'embarrassing failures of authenticity' that Bill Nichols cites as an almost inevitable effect of re-enactment. The hall runner scene is an interesting case. The point of the scene is supposed to be that straightening out the hall runner at 800 Ellice was a Sisyphean task that frustrated the entire family for years. Yet 'The actors put in a limp performance, displaying little affect.' The narration suggests that Maddin the director is frustrated in his very attempt to film a scene that conveys frustration. If re-enactment inevitably assigns more value to the recreated event than it is worth, it also makes us rethink our terms. If the focus shifts from 'what really happened' to 'what we think happened,' that is not so bad, because the question then becomes one of what such thoughts mean for us in the present.[24]

Something else to consider about the hall runner scene is that the movie is playing a shell game with the audience, albeit one that is conducted with a lot of winking and nudging. The narration informs us that the director has hired actors to play the roles of his siblings, that Spanky the pug is standing in for Toby the chihuahua, and that, in place of Maddin's dead father (and, as a homage to his first film, *The Dead Father*), there is a mound of earth under a rug to suggest that his corpse has been exhumed and reburied in the living room. Yet the narration also tells us: 'Mother is resistant to playing the role of herself in this exciting experiment of mine.' Anyone who has been exposed to even the most cursory of its reviews or Maddin's interviews before seeing *My Winnipeg* would know that the role of Mother is being played by Ann Savage, the most renowned actor in the film.

After much fighting and resistance from Mother, though, the narrator claims it begins to work: 'Mother is in the moment.' The failure of the runner-straightening project, the frustration and blockage that Maddin expresses to Michael Ondaatje about the hallway itself – 'And so it really did seem like nothing else went on in that hallway. I don't remember using the hallway to get from one room to the other. It just seemed to be the locus of irritation'[25] – is what allows the fantasy to temporarily succeed. The moment is an impasse: director, audience, and actor all recognize the lie; even the narrator seems convinced. In pretending to pretend that Ann Savage is playing his mother, Maddin gives her a role that is actually more real than reality; she becomes Mother. 'The Mother of All Interviews,' a fantasy scenario in the annotated script in which Herdis Maddin (the director's biological mother) and Ann Savage conduct a mutual interview, which, of course, is all about Guy and his various inadequacies, could end in only one way: a *mise en abyme*, with Ann Savage proclaiming, 'Hell, I'm ready to marry Guy and start calling you … *Mother!*' Accompanying 'The Mother of All Interviews' is a photograph of Herdis sitting in Maddin's living room, looking at a TV on which Ann Savage's face appears … as though she were staring into a mirror.[26]

Another point at which fantasy explicitly enters into *My Winnipeg* is through its animated sequences. Andy Smetanka, the animator, has been to Winnipeg once, and then for only a few days. His primary visual reference for the images he constructed was *Winnipeg 100*, a souvenir book of photographs published in 1973 for the province's centennial, which was sent to him by Maddin (Ironically, it was the book in which Smetanka found the If Day reference and brought it to the attention of Maddin, a former photo archivist.) 'I don't recall a single bit of Winnipeg architecture firsthand,' he writes. '*Winnipeg 100* had pages of long-gone schools and breweries, ginger-bread city halls and fabulous flatiron luxury motels, and in my creative megalomania I got it in my head to restore these vanished skylines to *My Winnipeg*, to resurrect them in silhouette for elderly residents bussed to the theatre from senior centres and managed-care facilities.'[27] The audience Smetanka imagines for his work is a fiction. All the animated sequences he produced for *My Winnipeg* are meticulously detailed, sharp-edged silhouettes against vivid, coloured backgrounds. In the context of a different movie, introducing a second degree of artificiality into the film via animation might, in contrast, make the fictional world of the rest of the film cohere in a kind of reality effect. In a film that already employs a golf bag full of visual styles, the animation takes its place as another heterogeneous element in the overall assemblage.

It is out of these seemingly endless doublings and redoublings that Maddin attempts not only to rethink his relationship to himself, but to populate a city. For Gilles Deleuze, in a documentary the director and characters become multiplicities together. The director replaces his fic-

The city as a mode of seeing: 'A Few of Winnipeg's Handsome Buildings.' Courtesy of Guy Maddin, from the director's personal collection.

tions with the stories he gleans from his subjects, but in the process of making a film, he transforms those ordinary stories into legends. Characters are filled with the director's words and desires, but the director also substitutes the anecdotes and stories of others for his own. This is the 'constitution or reconstitution of a people, where the film-maker and his characters become others together and the one through the other, a collectivity.'[28] Perhaps this is one reason Maddin portrays Winnipeg as a city of sleepwalkers and dreamers, with 'ten times the sleepwalking rate of any other city in the world.' Sleepwalkers and the hypnotized are vessels for something larger than themselves, some grand desire that might dictate their movement. At least, that is, until they encounter in their dreams some sort of traumatic truth that threatens the consistency of their fantasy, and they awake.

# More Ellipses:
# The City and Circulation

Winnipeg is not a city, it is a form of irony.

– Matthew Rankin[1]

In 1921, at the beginning of the decade whose films obsess Guy Maddin more than any other, poet and cultural critic Ezra Pound wrote the following incisive line for the *Dial*: 'In the city the visual impressions succeed each other, overlap, they are cinematographic.'[2] There have always been strong links between cinema and urban life, in ways that go far deeper than the observation that the city is a major theme in early film. In *The Country and the City*, Raymond Williams argues that 'there is indeed a direct relation between the motion picture, especially in its development in cutting and montage, and the characteristic movement of an observer in the close and miscellaneous environment of the streets.'[3] This leads Tony Pinkney to state that, for Williams, 'Film secretes the city in its very *form* long before it has ever announced it to us as an explicit theme ... and indeed, even if it does not address it specifically.'[4] There are deep structural similarities between film and the modern city, and each has much to do with bringing the other into being. James Donald's suggestion is that 'the city' is not so much a place as it is 'a historically specific mode of seeing,'[5] a set of practices, discourses, and technologies that organizes our perceptions and allows us to think about some aspect of the world in a particular way.

Michel de Certeau notes that the effect of 'the city' as a mode of seeing is to transform 'the urban *fact* into the *concept* of a city.' Interestingly, 'The desire to see the city preceded the means of satisfying it'; Renaissance painters employing perspective in their works were already showing the city in a manner that 'no eye had yet enjoyed.'[6] The city as a mode of seeing comes into its own in the late nineteenth century through media technologies such as photography, magic lantern shows, and panoramas, and through advances in engineering and architecture that allowed for the construction of taller buildings than ever before. Images of city life helped people to understand what it meant to be urban, and, by feeding the developing public taste for visual spectacle, paved the way for the arrival of cinema.[7] As Stephen Barber notes, cinema projection's audience in the first year of its existence, 1895, was almost entirely urban, as virtually all of the initial cinema showings occurred inside the bounds of cities.[8]

If 'the city' is a mode of seeing that appears along with the media technologies that employ it, what are its characteristic features? Barber's description of the very first work in the history of cinema is the logical starting point, which, he says, bears an 'outlandish simultaneity' to contemporary city films. In October 1888 Louis Le Prince shot a 3-second-long scene from a window overlooking the Leeds Bridge at the busiest moment of the day. In the background loom the grimy walls of Victorian hotels and warehouses. Pedestrians, carriages, and horse-drawn carts are crossing the bridge. Various small gestures are visible: a man wiping his nose, another tipping his hat to a woman passing by him, a woman carrying a package, conversations, and transactions, 'all of the elements capable of launching an intricate fiction film narrative are already prepared in those banal, scattered gestures.' Those human figures, like all bodies captured on film, are a confluence of the vital-

Guy Maddin's 'Berlin': (special) effects of the Real. Courtesy of Guy Maddin, from the director's personal collection.

ity of living beings and of the overwhelming certainty that the people moving in this scene are long since dead and gone. Barber describes it as an image that is 'imbued with corporeal gestures and urban surfaces together with intimations of death and loss.'[9] All of the elements of urban cinema are already in place: the indifference of the built environment; the circulation of people, animals, vehicles, objects, commerce, and information; the emotional drama of human encounters.

In his essay 'Walking in the City' in *The Practice of Everyday Life*, Certeau presents the two contrasting strategies that modernity uses to represent the city using the classical figures of Daedalus deep in his artificial, mechanical labyrinth, and Icarus, soaring high above it. The Daedalian view shows the city as lived by its inhabitants at street level: a series of 'mobile and endless labyrinths' that channels its citizens blindly through its passages and byways. The collective moments through this labyrinth produce 'a manifold story that has neither author nor spectator, shaped out of fragments of trajectories and alterations of spaces.' This aspect of the city has 'a certain strangeness that does not surface, or whose surface is only its upper limit.'[10] It is the home of the specific dimension of the uncanny that Mladen Dolar argues emerges with modernity and 'constantly haunts it from the inside.'[11] The Icarian view comes into existence as part of an attempt to escape from the dark and irrational world of the streets. As James Donald notes, it is the legacy of Enlightenment thinking and desires to represent the city as an aerial panorama, transparent and readable, and thus the perfect object of rational government and urban planning.[12] Certeau's metaphor also implies, of course, that hubris and inevitable failure are built into this desire.

The problem is that the more the proponents of the rational, governable city try to disavow its seedy underside, the more it spreads elsewhere. The progressive, Icarian perspective 'repeatedly produces effects contrary to those at which it aims: the profit system generates a loss which, in the multiple forms of wretchedness and poverty outside the system and of waste inside it, constantly turns production into "expenditure."' This is due to the fact that both perspectives are part of the same structure. Certeau identifies three registers that, in combination, allow us to make sense of the city: the believable, the memorable, and the primitive.[13] The believable (roughly equivalent to the Symbolic in Lacanian psychoanalysis) consists of the rational discourses and tactics that we use to construct the reality of the city for ourselves. This is the domain of Daedalus. The memorable (roughly equivalent to the Lacanian Imaginary) is the realm of memories and fantasies, both good and bad. About the primitive, which consists of pre-Symbolic infantile experience, Certeau says little, but the best analogy for it is the Lacanian Real.

The point of such a tripartite structure is that our sense of reality is based on a delicate balance between rationality (the Symbolic/believable/Daedalus) and fantasy (the Imaginary/memorable/Icarus). Rationality depends on at least a minimal amount of memory and fantasy for its consistency, enlisting them to paper over the cracks in our world view and protect us from the trauma of the Real (the blazing sun that melts the delicate wax-and-feather confection of Icarus's wings/the brute fact of one life's insignificance in a vast, impersonal city). 'The problem is that our most common experience of reality requires for its consistency a minimal share of regulative Ideas, of principles with reach beyond possible experience. In other words, the real choice is not the choice between naïve realism and delirious ghost-seeing, since, at a certain point, *they are both on the same side*: or, as Lacan would put it, there is no reality without its fantasmatic support.'[14] The governable city attempts to bring itself into being by denying the labyrinthine city, but the latter is as tenacious and inextricable as Edward Hyde is to Henry Jekyll – the destruction of the labyrinthine aspect of the city would destroy the city itself. In effect, the governable city is haunted by the labyrinthine city, whether it likes it or not.

This structure also holds true for cinema. As Carsten Strathausen remarks, 'the uncanny is literally built into both the metropolis and the cinematic apparatus.' Not only is the space of the movie theatre the literal dark spot in the heart of the city 'where modernity negotiated and tried to come to terms with its contradictory impulses of repression and revelation, transparency and obscurity,' but one of the functions of cinema is always 'to reanimate the dead and literally grant "life" to the mere shadows of photographic images.'[15]

What I'd like to suggest is that there is also a strong affinity between the interests of the governable city and the documentary on one hand, and the labyrinthine city and melodrama on the other. Moreover, within one of the filmic genres of the 1920s – the city symphony or 'cross-section'– documentary and melodrama coexist in dynamic tension. Both pragmatic reality testing and the combination of memory and imagination are necessary to produce 'the city' of modernity. Within the genre, various films tend more towards one pole or the other, but the aspects of any city symphony that film critics emphasize change as cultural discourse changes over time. For example, Donald argues that Siegfried Kracauer's first review of *Man with Movie Camera* in the *Frankfurter Zeitung* in 1929 did not emphasize the qualities that might interest us today, such as its revolutionary perspective or its technophilia, but focused instead on 'its affinity with states of dreaming and dying.'[16] Before we return directly to *My Winnipeg*, then, it is time to take a detour through the neighbourhoods of the city symphony.

From Louis Le Prince's 3-second film of Leeds onward, films whose sum and substance are depictions of the city have always been a significant presence in cinema. In the first two decades of the twentieth century, examples of city films abound. Scott MacDonald lists *Panorama Water Front and Brooklyn and Bridge from East River* (1903) and *New York City 'Ghetto' Fish Market* (1903), both produced by Thomas Edison, as two prominent early examples of city films.[17] Many others could easily be

71

added to this list, including James White's *Paris Exposition Films* for the Edison Manufacturing Company (1900), Frederick S. Armitage's *Demolishing and Building Up the Star Theatre* (1901), Robert K. Bonine's *Lower Broadway* (1902) and *Beginning of a Skyscraper* (1902), J.B. Smith's *Skyscrapers of NYC from North River* (1903), G.W. 'Billy' Bitzer's *Panorama from the Tower of the Brooklyn Bridge* (1903) and *Interior New York Subway, 14th Street to 42nd Street* (1905), Wallace McCutcheon's *Panorama from Times Building, New York* (1905), Edwin S. Porter's *Coney Island At Night* (1905), and various others shot between 1899 and 1924. (Many of these films have been collected in *Picturing A Metropolis: New York City Unveiled*, disc 5 of the excellent collection *Unseen Cinema: Early American Avant-Garde Film, 1894–1941*.)

City symphonies proper begin to appear in the early 1920s. In the list of films that are usually cited as belonging to this genre, among the most frequently appearing are Charles Sheeler and Paul Strand's *Manhatta* (1921), Alberto Cavalcanti's *Rien que les Heures / Nothing But the Hours* (1926), Karl Freund's *Die Abenteuer Eines Zehnmarkscheins / The Adventures of a Ten-Mark Note* (1926), Jean Vigo's *À propos de Nice* (1926), Walter Ruttmann's *Berlin: die Sinfonie einer Grossstadt / Berlin: Symphony of a Great City* (1927), Dziga Vertov's *Cheloveks kino-apparatom / Man with the Movie Camera* (1929), Herman Weinberg's lost film, *A City Symphony* (1930), and Manoel de Oliveira's *Douro, Faina fluvial / Working on the Douro River* (1931). The best known of these films, and those that had the most direct influence on Maddin, are Ruttmann's *Berlin* and Vertov's *Man with the Movie Camera*.

Siegfried Kracauer called these films 'cross-sections' after the term that Béla Balázs, scriptwriter for Freund's *The Adventures of a Ten-Mark Note*, devised for his work, the notion being that such a film would touch on all aspects of city life, as experienced by all classes of people. Though Kracauer sees Freund's film as the embryonic form of an idea that be fully realized by Ruttman and Vertov, he makes an interesting remark: 'The documentary character of the cross-section pattern is blurred by its combination with a sentimental Berlin local drama concerning a worker and a factory girl.' While Kracauer insists that the rapid montage-based editing style of these later directors, which focuses on 'formal qualities of objects rather than their meanings' and 'pure patterns of movement' rather than human stories is the essence of this new genre,[18] later critics who have abandoned the notion of teleology of form will note that sentimental drama, even melodrama, is inextricable from the abstract, inhuman aspect of the city symphony genre. With this in mind, it is possible to enlarge this list to account for the other end of the spectrum by including fiction films from the same period in which the city still serves as a main character, such as Harold Lloyd's *Safety Last!* (1923), Fritz Lang's *Metropolis* (1927), King Vidor's *The Crowd* (1928), and, on the outside edge, Charles Chaplin's *City Lights* (1931) and *Modern Times* (1936). Many of the genre's conventions were also used in later films to tell different kinds of stories: the detective films and noir films from the 1940s and 1950s bear a strong kinship to the city symphony, as do the cyberpunk-tinged science fiction films of the 1980s and 1990s.

Scott MacDonald's summary of the city symphony form is as good as any: these films provide 'choreographed depictions of a representative day in the life of the modern city from before dawn until after dark.'[19] The aesthetics of city cinema are the logical outcome of the possibilities of montage, a manifold array of perspectives cut together in a rapid, rhythmic manner.[20] As a result, the action in city symphonies is rarely constructed according to anything resembling a plot; 'image association and not causal logic often determine[s] the order of shots.'[21] Historically, one of the reason for the popularity of these films was their relationship to the 'cinema of attractions' in early film. The novelty of the city symphony's accelerated montage produced visceral thrills in an audience that was still watching the language of cinema develop before their very eyes.[22] It is no slight to argue that some of the excitement around Maddin's films is also a result of the fact that he employs techniques that make his films look different from everyone else's.

Character works differently in city symphonies than in many other genres. Because of the central role of montage, often no one person is on the screen for very long, meaning that character development in any given shot's microplot (whether staged or happened upon – city symphonies rarely employ many professional actors) stays at a minimum. Various kinds of figures (the detective, the anthropologist, the *flâneur*, the director, a narrator) are capable of negotiating the genre's tension between the documentary and the dramatic, so when one figure does 'stick out' from the masses, these types predominate.[23] Nevertheless, the main 'character' is almost always the city itself.

To offset the reduced roles of plot and character, city symphonies invoke different kinds of continuity. This is often temporal continuity, where the action takes place in a set period of time, but it is important not to lose sight of the fact that montage, in conjunction with effects such as freeze frame, slow motion, and fast-forward, *constructs* the rhythms and thus the temporality in the film.[24] In other cases, the association that holds the city symphony together is spatial. The role of the film's title, which is often a direct reference to a specific place, helps to hold the entire assemblage together. Filmmakers have often used the form to experiment with 'the physique of the city' by cutting together shots of different and frequently 'incompatible' locations, manufacturing artificial landscapes that are only possible on screen. In keeping with the industrial ethos of the era that produced them, city symphonies are resolutely *manufactured* objects, 'less about documenting reality as reality is, and more about producing an artificial reality.'[25] James Donald observes that *Berlin* differs from Ruttmann's earlier abstract films by virtue of its inclusion of 'an almost voyeuristic record of the little human dramas of public life. Children go to school, people chat in cafés, a policeman helps a little boy across the road, prostitutes ply their trade, street performers appear in silly costumes, a woman commits suicide.'[26] The sudden melodrama of the suicide sequence features tight close-ups of the stark, staring eyes of a woman leaning over the edge of a bridge, intercut with shots from a camera fixed to the front car of a roller coaster and spinning disks with spiral designs on them, followed a by a shot of rippling water at the base of the bridge. For a moment, the suicide sequence punctures the film's abstract patterns and rhythms, sending ripples of affect back through the footage we have already seen and forward through the images yet to come. Though it does not overwhelm the rest of the film, the scene remains fixed in the viewer's imagination as a troubling reminder of the human cost of modernity's speed and power.

One of Kracauer's other points is also useful for our purposes. When contrasting *Man with the Movie Camera* with *Berlin*, he remarks that the basic difference in the meaning of these films is a result of the application of 'similar aesthetic principles to the rendering of dissimilar worlds.' Vertov produces 'a reality quivering with revolutionary energies' whereas for him, Ruttmann's film, which employs many of the same techniques, presents 'a shapeless reality, one that seems to be abandoned by all vital energies.'[27] When Maddin takes the aesthetic conventions of the city symphony and applies them to a city that differs drastically in time as well as place from the European cities of the 1920s and early 1930s, we can and should expect further dislocations in terms of the meanings that these conventions produce.

From the outset of the *My Winnipeg* project, Maddin has been explicit about working within the city symphony genre, and about the influence of Ruttmann and Vertov on his film's aesthetic (he has a copy of the famous *Man with the Movie Camera* poster hanging in his kitchen). In his piece on the origins of *My Winnipeg*, Denis Seguin writes, 'Maddin envisioned a production along the lines of Walter Ruttmann's *Berlin: Symphony of a Great City*, a 1927 film that captured a day in the life of that distant pre-war city.'[28] What practically no reviewers who have mentioned the link between Ruttmann's film and Maddin's have noticed is that, just before he made *My Winnipeg*, Guy Maddin also made a tiny city symphony called ... *Berlin.*

Maddin's *Berlin* (2007) is a 1-minute-long 16mm black and white film made out of found footage and distributed on DVD with *My Winnipeg*. It was produced for the Kitchener-Waterloo Art Gallery's Parochial View series, which consists of 'Artist's reflections on our urban and rural environs through a series of commissioned works.' Originally settled by a largely German immigrant population, Kitchener, Ontario, was known as the Town of Berlin from 1854 to 1912 and the City of Berlin from 1912 to 1916. As World War I loomed and anti-German sentiment rose, other Canadians began to express growing doubts about whether or not the people of Berlin were doing everything they could to support the British war effort. The hurling of a bust of Kaiser Wilhelm II into the lake in Victoria Park, an infamous event in the city's history that occurred not once but twice before the bust disappeared completely, was a decidedly Maddin-like event, which, sadly, did not make it into the film.

As part of their attempt to improve the city's image in the eyes of other Canadians, in 1916 the city changed its name to Kitchener, in honour of the popular British secretary of state for war. In May 1916, the city council also hired Charlie Roos, a filmmaker from the nearby town of Galt, to produce a 15-minute propaganda film. Roos and his cameraman filmed the largely German-descended soldiers of the 118th Battalion at its barracks at Queen South and Courtland, marching along Queen and King streets, conducting drills in Victoria Park, and receiving $10 gold coins from the city, all in preparation for going to fight the citizens of their ancestral homeland. Roos also attached a camera to a streetcar running down King Street and shot footage of the Berlin fire department. The completed film included a gun-firing scene from another war movie Roos was making in Galt. The original has since been lost,

Ann Savage, force of Nature (director's caption). Courtesy of Guy
Maddin, from the director's personal collection.

but some of Roos's footage was saved by William Musclow, long-time projectionist at the Lyric Theatre, and then given to the *Kitchener-Waterloo Record*. The newspaper had it transferred from silver-nitrate to a 16mm safety positive, which became Maddin's raw material.[29] Because of the constraints of the commission – the final film had to be 1 minute long – Maddin and John Gurdebecke's interventions consist primarily of editing, the addition of a soundtrack, their unique 'scrolling' editing technique, and the occasional appearance of the word 'BERLIN.' Nevertheless, from the initial train track footage onward, Maddin's film meets enough of the generic requirements that it can at least be considered one movement in a city symphony, and perhaps, even better, as an overture for *My Winnipeg*.

The difference in time and place between *My Winnipeg* and the city symphonies of the 1920s and 1930s means that, despite Maddin's employment of many of the genre's conventions, the relative balance between pragmatic reality testing and fantasy has shifted. Where classic examples of the city symphony genre such as *Berlin* or *Man with the Movie Camera* consist largely of the believable, with the memorable enlisted to support it against incursions of the primitive, Maddin's *My Winnipeg* dwells largely in memory and fantasy, with the believable playing a secondary role and traumatic moments of the primitive leaking out to a greater extent than in the majority of other city symphonies. Jim Hoberman writes, 'Making his own detours, Maddin transforms Winnipeg into a city of mystery. No less than Feuillade's Paris, this is a dream dump of labyrinthine alleyways, mysterious monuments, and peculiar landmarks.'[30] In a city symphony made in the 1920s, melodrama might suddenly intrude in order to bring the implicit, imaginary subtext or dream logic to the surface.[31] In *My Winnipeg*, we dwell in dream and melodrama and wonder constantly if the believable will even *remain* believable for long. In Maddin's filmic world, it is often the fabrications that are most believable and the historical facts that seem preposterous.

As in examples of the city symphony from the 1920s, the structure of *My Winnipeg* is metonymic and associational rather than narrative. Like the giant Wolseley Elm growing out of the centre of a tiny circular boulevard in the middle of the Avenue, there are small islands of plot in *My Winnipeg*, connected by the meandering desires, recollections and daydreams of the director. 'Stories about places,' writes Michel de Certeau, 'are makeshift things. They are composed of the world's debris.' Such stories, consisting of fragments of text tied to half-remembered family histories, urban legends, overheard conversations, personal anecdotes, and pillow talk, are articulated by their gaps as much as by their substance: 'everywhere punched and torn open by ellipses, drifts, and leaks of meaning: it is a sieve-order.'[32] For his part, Maddin says, 'for months before I began filming *My Winnipeg*, I had a Post-It note on my fridge reading 'More Ellipses.'[33] In exchange for the certainties of plot, what such a structure affords are entrances and exits, the possibility of escape, and perhaps even of return, but always a trajectory towards a way of telling things that differs from the official one.

One route into a film that has no overarching plot to describe and no 'round' characters to analyse is to consider the route itself as part of a larger circulatory system. Both thematically and formally, *My Winnipeg* is a film that is deeply concerned with circulation from the first words of the narration – 'All aboard!' – onward.

On a thematic level, *My Winnipeg* concerns almost nothing *but* circulation. In an email to Andy Smetanka, Maddin describes the construction of a multi-purpose prop that drives this point home: 'Right now I'm having built a multi-purpose prop which serves as a light-table, a map of Winnipeg and its river forks which suggest the subterranean forks directly beneath, a pair of intersecting train tracks on snow, and a pair of crossed follopian [*sic*] tubes in the menstruating lap of my mother. Not being able to find this item at the local Giant Tiger, I'm forced to pay union coin for its construction! Woe!'[34]

*My Winnipeg* scrapbook cover by animator Andy Smetanka. Courtesy of Guy Maddin, from the director's personal collection.

The train tracks in and out of Winnipeg, the 'arteries' and 'iron veins' of the film's opening monologue, allude to the city's geographical placement in the centre of the continent and to its waning importance as a twentieth-century transportation and communication hub, especially for grain. The famous 'forks' of the Red and Assiniboine rivers invoke an earlier transportation system used by the First Nations and the Métis, the Hudson's Bay Company, voyageurs, explorers, and police from the east, as well as the nexus of settlement, the Riel Rebellion, and the eventual founding of the province – there is an entire political economy of the city embedded in this image alone. But as in the prop itself, Maddin continues to add layers to this circulatory palimpsest: the bridges that cross Winnipeg's rivers and railways, especially the Arlington Street Bridge, designed to span the Nile in Egypt and retrofitted for use over Winnipeg's rail yards; the city's streets and, especially, its back alleys; graveyards and morgues; vehicles such as taxis, snowshoes, skates, and sleighs; the interiors of buildings and the systems that channel people and objects through them – hallways, urine troughs, swimming pools, schools, department stores, staircases, chambers in the legislature, cafeterias, hair chutes; and people themselves, as objects and vectors of legends, rumours, and anecdotes, and, in several cases, as literal 'mediums' for the voices and images of the dead.

The theme of circulation has always been a component of the city symphony, yet it too has been transfigured by the shift in time and place from 1920s Odessa and Berlin to Winnipeg in 2007. Wolfgang Natter emphasizes that by virtue of its focus on various aspects of urban infrastructure – systems to produce and distribute power, heat, and electricity and to manage the flows of traffic and sewage – Ruttmann's *Berlin*, like *My Winnipeg*, displays the city as a palimpsest of circulatory systems. However, if 'the street, as pure circulation and movement, defines the essence of the modern city,'[35] then Winnipeg's defining moment is the massive stoppage of all flows in the 1919 General Strike.

A consideration of circulation also involves taking into account block-ages, breakdowns, traffic jams, and other impediments, and dispersal and loss as well as accumulation. Lassitude. Amnesia. Invading Nazis. The death of loved ones. Buried rivers. Sharp objects heaving out of the frozen ground of Garbage Hill. Dynamited trees, demolished buildings, lost innocence, horses frozen in the icy crust of the river. And, over everything, endless and impenetrable blankets of ice, snow, and fog.

*My Winnipeg* presents the audience with a city of frozen architecture. Maddin claims in his annotations to the script that, after the opening of the Panama Canal and the resulting decline of Winnipeg as a transcon-tinental rail shipping hub, no new buildings have been constructed in the city's Exchange District since 1914.[36] More modern, efficient passag-es exist elsewhere than the heart of the heart of the country. The streets of Winnipeg are 'snow labyrinths' and 'mazes of ectoplasm,' clogged and confusing rather than bustling with activity. The narrator tells us the citizenry actually prefers to use 'the fine grid-like work of narrow unspoken-of byways' that is the back-lane system (complete with its own cab company), even though the lanes appear on no city maps. 'It's inside these black arteries where the real Winnipeg is found.' If Rutt-mann and Vertov distil the essence of the modernist governable city in *Berlin* and *Man with the Movie Camera*, then what *My Winnipeg* presents is not even its obverse, the labyrinthine city (of, say, *Metropolis* or *Blade Runner*). For all its darkness and its confusion, the labyrinthine city had its liberatory aspects. Maddin's Winnipeg, though, is a new configura-tion of the labyrinthine and the corrosive forces of the Real, where the pockets of liberation and excess become fewer and farther between.

The sequence on the train, which appears very near the beginning of *My Winnipeg*, is also a form whose meaning has been transfigured by the city symphony's redeployment far from its historical and geographic context. The first images of Berlin in the film from which the city sym-phony genre derives its name are also shot from a camera affixed to the front of a train. Stephen Barber remarks, 'That seminal arrival into the core of the city was replicated in innumerable city films of subsequent years,'[37] so its presence at the opening of *My Winnipeg* signals a generic kinship. It also prepares us for a particular kind of viewing experience. As Wolfgang Schivelbusch observed in *The Railway Journey*, by virtue of the train's large, panoramic windows, the passenger on the train almost immediately became the equivalent of the modern viewer in a movie theatre.[38]

In his writing on cinema, Gilles Deleuze calls this ordinary viewer 'the man without qualities' after Robert Musil's famous book – an epithet that Maddin took for himself in his treatment 'The Child without Qualities,' sections of which have appeared throughout the Me Trilogy, including *My Winnipeg*. For Deleuze, what the ordinary viewers see in shots like those of the train track alone or, better yet, in a rapid montage between shots, is pure movement, and in that image they recognize themselves. Deleuze writes that this movement-image 'does not reproduce a world, but constitutes an autonomous world, made up of breaks and disproportion, deprived of all its centres, addressing itself as such to a viewer who is in himself no longer centre of his own perception.'[39] Modern cinema in which the movement-image plays a central part takes time as its subject matter. In this cinema, the connections between actions and perceptions are broken. Space no longer coheres; it becomes the sieve-like structure that Certeau describes, populated by vague, nomadic characters in thrall to the tedium of the everyday.[40]

Again, this function of the train shot in early city symphonies continues to hold true for *My Winnipeg*, to a degree. Like the other images of circulation, though, it too has been transfigured in significant ways. In a contemporary context, particularly in a Canada where funding cuts have stripped the formerly dense national passenger train service down to a few thin lines, it would have made perfect sense to begin with an aerial shot of the city as an airplane landed. Instead, making the train the transit system of choice leaves the city as something to be explored from the perspective of someone already within the labyrinth, depriving the audience of the privilege of a comprehensive birds-eye view. Still, the train tracks themselves are solid, industrial, believable, Symbolic.

There are two characteristics of the train sequence of *My Winnipeg* that are particularly worthy of comment. The first is that the figure in the shot is asleep. I write 'the figure' because the role is unmentioned in the film's credits, and Maddin is quick to point this out, unprompted, during an interview.[41] Nevertheless, the camera's focus on the sleeping figure while the narrator, also the director, uses the first-person pronoun, sutures the 'I' to this figure. In addition, the part is played by Darcy Fehr, who also plays 'Guy Maddin' in *Cowards Bend the Knee*. Also, like 'Guy Maddin, house painter' who first appears asleep in a boat in the opening of *Brand Upon the Brain!*, this figure first appears asleep in vehicle. According to Maddin's note in the annotated script, Darcy Fehr 'sits in for me in the train-carriage sequences,'[42] but this only adds to the confusion, because of Maddin's avowed preference for telling different interviewers that different aspects of the film are true. Denis Seguin begins his piece on *My Winnipeg* with the sentences 'Guy Maddin is a liar, and he knows it. His colleagues and collaborators know it' for a reason.[43]

Despite the long tradition of beginning city films with train sequences, this one was added as a pick-up shot after initial filming had been completed. Maddin relates the following to Zachary Wigon at the Tribeca Film Festival:

> I was lying in a couch in Los Angeles watching TCM and a Sherlock Holmes movie. I think it was called *Terror on the Train* or something. I don't know what it was [ed. note: *Terror by Night*]. The whole thing takes place on a train and I realized that Winnipeg is there because of the trains. I love train movies. Trains are very sleepy and dreamy things. And a little

bit claustrophobic – my preferred style of shooting. So I just realized I had to, as annoying as it was to my producer ... I had to go back and have a train set built and cram a bunch of people in and just shoot this sort of framing device. So the *I Vitelloni* thing eventually got replaced by a train thing, something to make everything sort of cohere.[44]

The triple repetition of phrases and words evokes the hypnotic rhythms of train travel. This is also a convention found in other films, such as the opening sequence of Lars von Trier's *Europa* (1991), which begins with a shot of train tracks and the voice of a hypnotist intoning 'I shall now count from one to ten.'

The salient difference between the train sequence in *My Winnipeg* and the city symphonies inspired by *Berlin* is that the train in Maddin's film is *leaving* the city – or at least *attempting* to leave, because the narrator mentions 'many botched attempts.' In combination with the narration's emphasis on sleep, dream, and nostalgia, the overwhelming suggestion is that the 'where' in this film is imaginary ... which takes us to other layers of circulation altogether.

# The Forks beneath the Forks: Desire and Drive

I've always known my films were queer, just the way von Sternberg's films were queer.

– Guy Maddin[1]

When describing the quality of desire in Guy Maddin's films, Darrell Varga repeatedly resorts to metaphors of liquidity and flow. Despite all attempts to block or channel its flow in the name of polite society and its mores, desire is forever 'bubbling over.'[2] If *My Winnipeg* is a film that is concerned with circulation on a variety of levels, the force that loosely connects the entire assemblage is indeed *affective* circulation: the agitated emotions, memories, drives, and desires of the director. 'Winnipeg. Winnipeg, Winnipeg': the obsessive repetition of the film's narration, beginning with these words, suggests the characteristic spiral structure of drive.[3] 'I must leave it. I must leave it. I must leave it now,' the narration continues, but the desire for escape always fails. The narrator can never truly leave Winnipeg behind, because his subjectivity is organized around it. If *My Winnipeg* is a documentary, perhaps what it documents is the transformation of the panic and lassitude of being trapped in a single city for one's entire life into the energy that allows for the production not just of a work of art, but of an entire oeuvre.

Maddin's claim that his films are queer in 'just the way von Stern-berg's were queer' is one route into the topic of desire and its circulation. It suggests that Maddin conceives of queerness in much the same way that Jack Babuscio does in 'Camp and the Gay Sensibility,' his essay in the landmark collection *Camp Grounds: Style and Homosexuality*. Using director Josef von Sternberg as a specific example, Babuscio describes a set of relationships between 'activities, individuals, situations *and* gayess' that can be accessed and invoked even by subjects who do not explicitly identify as gay.[4] Likewise, Nikki Sullivan's *A Critical Introduction to Queer Theory* describes queerness in terms of its specific relationship towards flows of desire, as a process that strives 'to make strange, to frustrate, to counteract, to delegitimise, to camp up – heteronormative knowledges and institutions, and the subjectivities and socialities that are (in)formed by them and (in)form them.'[5]

From this perspective, queerness manifests itself in film not simply as a group of themes about sexuality, but as a set of techniques. Darragh O'Donoghue's 'Particles of Illusion: Guy Maddin and His Precursors' documents how Von Sternberg's erotic obsessions, blendings of fantasy and autobiography, and cruel ironies (all elements of what would later be dubbed a camp sensibility) became inextricable from a range of formal qualities as a result of the editing process for *Der Blaue Engel/The Blue Angel* (1930):

In common with most early sound films, *Engel* was shot in different languages in a doomed attempt to retain silent cinema's global market. However, few of the cast could speak German, and those that did (with the exception of Marlene Dietrich) were incomprehensible. What had been a sombre film of perfect dramatic unity was travestied by long stretches of untranslated German, poor lip-synching, clunky cuts, stiff performances, churns, hisses and gaps on the soundtrack, and abrupt switches in the film's stock, as English dialogue scenes were inserted

into the German 'original.' Further, some character and plot information was eliminated (the English version is 12 minutes shorter), creating
unnecessary confusion in a story that can't explain why Germans insist
on speaking to each other in bad English.

O'Donoghue notes that while these effects were created by an editor
other than von Sternberg, the director's later work 'would revel in disjunctive effects, not just in those films taken from him and reworked
by others.'[6] The 'queerness' of Maddin's films is an amalgam of sensi-
bilities and techniques that draw liberally on von Sternberg and others,
but it also has much to do with the specific editing process Maddin developed with John Gurdebecke (see chapter 8). While popular culture,
from shock-jock radio to YouTube to reality TV, is replete with examples
of campy 'content,' it is the coincidence of that content with far less
common disjunctive techniques – what Moe Meyer calls 'the signifying
practices that processually constitute queer identities'[7] – that creates
the potentially subversive element in Maddin's work.

While it is arguable that Maddin's films are queer in terms of their
technique, and the director himself uses the notion of queerness to
describe his sensibility, it is more accurate to describe the male relationships that they depict as *homosocial* rather than homosexual. I am using
the term 'homosociality' here in the sense that Eve Kosofsky Sedgwick
uses it in her influential book *Between Men: English Literature and Male Homosocial Desire*. In the social sciences, Sedgwick remarks, the term 'homosocial' refers to social bonds between people of the same sex, but it
is not a synonym for 'homosexual.' In such contexts, she observes, the
term usually refers to activities like male bonding, which can just as
easily be profoundly homophobic as loving and affirmative. Sedgwick's
project is 'to draw the "homosocial" back into the orbit of "desire,"' that
is, to re-establish a continuum between the homosocial and the homosexual, allowing for the possibility of a libidinal charge in relations

between all men, regardless of their sexual practices or object choice, without fear of homophobic reprisal.[8] One of the signature characteristics of Maddin's films, both in *My Winnipeg* and in shorts such as *Sissy Boy Slap Party* (2004) and *Glorious* (2008), is precisely this sort of utopian homosociality. What makes a difference is the positive value that Maddin places on homosociality in *My Winnipeg* and elsewhere in his work.

Maddin's filmmaking history traces an arc from some of the more problematic examples of homosociality to a positive erotics of male friendship very similar to the one that Sedgwick describes. Maddin and his Drone friends, John Boles Harvie in particular, explicitly claim to have started making films to pick up dates.[9] Once he actually started showing his films to audiences of any substantial size, though, Maddin noticed that 'the people sticking around for Q-and-As weren't girls. I had the middle-aged queen set cornered. I enjoyed it, though, because we'd go out for drinks afterwards and they could talk film. A noble and rewarding demographic.'[10] As this movement from eros (communication to one intended lover) to rhetoric (communication to many) also hews closely to the structure of the *Phaedrus* of Plato's Socrates, we can, after John Durham Peters, read both moments in Maddin's career as deviations from 'a normative grid of communications.' Instead of the laudable normative modes that Plato's Socrates presents, personal eros and public rhetoric, what Maddin describes inverts these terms. Eros is ostensibly intensely personal, but Maddin and his friends practise a kind of mass Eros. The 'shy, homely theatre girls' that Maddin brags about are addressed as unique individuals and signed to movie contracts drafted on the back of cocktail napkins from the bars they'd just left,[11] as though they have something special to offer, but really are members of an entire class of possible lovers. Conversely, rhetoric is supposed to be public, crafted for a mass audience. Maddin's films and memoirs move in the opposite direction: intensely and embarrassingly personal, they are loved by perfect strangers who are well versed in film history. For Plato, neither mode is satisfactory; the possibilities of interpersonal communication thus remain in a deadlock.[12] From Plato's Socrates to Guy Maddin, the history of communication is also always a history of communication's failure.

For Maddin, the bonds of male friendship constitute a circuit that circulates and transmutes two important kinds of objects: libidinal energy and potential plot material, in the form of ideas, anecdotes, forgotten facts, tall tales, and good-natured lies of the sort that Robert Kroetsch, the prairie poet laureate of the homosocial, fondly refers to as 'bullshit.'[13] Maddin's references to Winnipeg filmmaker and actor Noam Gonick, for example, inevitably both emphasize his importance to Maddin's creative process and further mythologize Gonick's own sexual prowess. (See also 'Happy Ever After,' Maddin's interview with Gonick about his film *Hey, Happy!* [2001]).[14] Crucially, one of the 'half-remembered' local myths that Gonick supplies Maddin with on their night-time strolls is the template for the circulation of desire that runs throughout *My Winnipeg*: 'The forks beneath the Forks: an old tale from the First Nations has it that there are subterranean forks, two secret rivers meeting, directly beneath the Assiniboine and the Red, this double pair of rivers being extra supernaturally powerful.'[15] Its veracity, like that of every other factoid in the film, is beside the point. The phrase 'old tale' marks this level as falling well within the zone of legend and dream.

Maddin has also claimed that Gonick came by the story from a First Nations man he was trying to seduce.[16] As I have discussed elsewhere, throughout the history of Manitoba, the First Nations and the Métis have lived out the experience of liminality, literally relegated to the marginal spaces of reserves, of narrow strips of road allowances between the farms of settlers, or as part of the urban poor. During the 1970s and 1980s Winnipeg's male prostitutes, some of whom were First Nations and Métis, gathered along the banks of the Assiniboine River (lending some credence to the seduction anecdote) behind both the Manitoba and, ironically, the original home of Étienne Gaboury and Marcien Lemay's controversial statue of Louis Riel.[17] Moreover, as Terry Goldie argues throughout *Fear and Temptation: The Image of the Indigene in Canadian, Australian, and New Zealand Literatures*, images of indigenous peoples in colonial cultures personify the mix of white attraction and repulsion to both the indigenes and the land itself.[18]

The few images of first peoples in *My Winnipeg* are certainly ambivalent, but it is arguable that the film constitutes a critique of their forced liminality in its desire for something better. Maddin's narrator imagines the First Nations as part of 'those swelling ranks of our heartsick dispossessed' who gather up the detritus of Happyland, Winnipeg's long, last, winter carnival palace, and from 'every last sliver of happiness' they can gather, they reconstitute it 'out of sight up on the rooftops of our city, above us, an Aboriginal Happyland.' This is not so much a forced marginalization as it is what Hakim Bey might call a TAZ – a Temporary Autonomous Zone where non-normative desires might be enacted and revolutions planned.[19] Nevertheless, when Citizen Girl, Maddin's Marxist pin-up, arrives to 'tend to those in our aerial Happyland' and right all the wrongs of the past, she is unambiguously white, leaving salvation, once again, in the hands of the colonizers.

The few overtly utopian spaces that exist within *My Winnipeg*, such as the dressing room of the Maroons in the Winnipeg Arena, the Paddlewheel restaurant during the mythical Golden Boy pageants of the 1940s, and the third and lowest of the Sherbrook swimming pool, all have a homosocial quality.[20] Swimming serves Maddin in much the same way that walking does, as a form of exercise, an opportunity for homosocial bonding, and a space for ruminating on issues pertaining to various film projects. In *From the Atelier Tovar*[21] and in conversation with William Beard, the director makes particular mention of swimming with Steve Snyder, one of Maddin's early inspirations and a long-

Sherbrook Pool boy's shower room maquette. Courtesy of Guy Maddin, from the director's personal collection.

time confidant and adviser: 'I would discuss my bad relationship with him while doing the dog paddle up and down for an hour and just try to figure out ways of making *The Hands of Orloc* [*sic*] work.'[22] In *My Winnipeg* itself, the three underground levels of the Sherbrook Pool apparently are segregated by gender, not to block illicit desires, but to enable them. As the narrator announces that the second level was for 'girls only,' the film shows a shot of two young girls practising artificial respiration, then eroticizes it by using of an intertitle exclaiming 'Girls on girls!' In comparison with the attention lavished on the third, boys-only level, though, this scene receives short shrift. 'It was always rumoured the water in the boys' pool came directly from the Forks beneath the Forks,' observes the narrator, attributing this flow of liquid desire as the 'mystical power' behind the 'Dance of the Hairless Boners' that takes place as the grade 5 boys turn their locker room into a prepubescent bacchanal. The 'What If's in the narration that follow the disappearance of these zones are a testament to the ambivalent power of the Imaginary to construct new possible worlds ... but only when posed as a question, not as a positive statement.

The third layer of Maddin's multipurpose circulatory prop is directly and unambiguously linked to maternal sexuality, which functions according to another logic altogether. When the narrative repetition slips into 'The forks, the lap. The forks, the lap. The forks, the lap,' there is no doubt that *My Winnipeg*'s obsession with the site of Maddin's own production is literal, beginning with the fallopian tubes in his mother's lap. This is the realm of the Real, of primitive prelinguistic drive, continually pulling the narrator back to the place of origin from his wanderings.

On the level of content, the maternal lap sequences at the opening of the film are only mildly scandalous, imposing a screen of a woman's pubic mound over the map of the forks. Maddin mischievously attempts to elicit further scandal at the expense of both his mother and his ex in the film's annotated script: 'I've often said the hardest part of shooting *My Winnipeg* was tugging the girdle off my mom for these nude shots of a female lap. But almost everyone believes these snug thighs belong to my ex-girlfriend, Erin Hershberg. I promised her I would set the record straight in these notes: I do hereby swear that the naked lap in *My Winnipeg* does not belong to Erin Hershberg!'[23] For the curious, the photograph is of the lap of a professional life model who regularly poses for art classes at the University of Manitoba.[24] But the invocation of his ex-girlfriend's nude lap is only a screen for the film's real obsession, 'the lap of my mother.'

Whenever heterosexual desire appears in *My Winnipeg*, a maternal figure is always close at hand to police it. When the narrator begins to fantasize about the 'solicitous schoolgirls' of St. Mary's Academy fondling and kissing him, reality intrudes 'with the arrival of a big nun.' This frustrated fantasy segues immediately into a dialogue between Mother and the narrator's sister Janet, who has just hit a deer while driving back to Winnipeg from Kenora. Mother acts as a kind of rogue psychoanalyst, seeing past the 'fur and blood' on the car's fender to the intercourse between her daughter and the 'man with the tire iron' who put the injured deer out of its misery. 'Mother, she knows how to read all the signs,' muses the narrator. 'Those gentle substitutions for dark wishes.' Moreover, he generalizes this experience outward, to include all Winnipeggers: 'She can read our family and our civic secrets, our desire and our shame, as easily as she can read a newspaper.' From Mother's perspective, the standard narratives of desire and seduction are simply illusions to brush aside. For the narrator and the city alike, this is a first step in confronting a deeper trauma.

Darrell Varga's essay on *Careful* suggests that, whenever the flows of desire in Maddin's films approach the maternal body, a necessary process of veiling occurs. 'Maddin's films are literally shot through with veils, are about the fact of veiling, are decidedly not a narrative trajectory toward the unveiling of meaning. Images abound of the maternal

All aboard! Courtesy of Guy Maddin, from the director's personal collection.

bed draped in translucent fabric though which the desirous boy must penetrate and in which he inevitably becomes entangled.'[25] This maternal veiling is not merely a recurring image or theme. Maddin has also realized it on the level of technique by shooting through a scrim made from his mother's underwear to cast a gauzy haze over his camera lens (a photo of Maddin doing exactly this on the set of *Odilon Redon* appears in Caelum Vatnsdal's *Kino Delirium*).[26] In effect, it is an attempt to use desire supported by fantasy as a screen to occlude the abyss of the Thing, the sublime object that lies beyond it.[27] Maddin uses exactly this vocabulary to refer to Ann Savage's on-screen presence once he begins to film her as Mother: 'Shocking was the power of her visage still, at age eighty-seven, enhaloed as it was in eerie ectoplasms, her presence an uncanny *it* imperiously demanding its rightful third dimension as it spectrally wafted – no, loomed threateningly – out toward her beholders.'[28]

But the approach that psychoanalysis employs to effect a cure for this endless circling of the maternal Thing, called 'traversing the fantasy,' takes a radically different path, abandoning the hope of escape and fully assuming the weight of this 'eternal return.'[29] The genius of *My Winnipeg* is that it does exactly that, transforming the excessive pressures of drive into force to power its creative engines. 'The point is not that artists reconcile the opposites and tensions in the aesthetic Totality of a harmonious Whole, but on the contrary, that they construct a place in which people can ecstatically perceive the traumatic excesses around which their life turns.'[30] *My Winnipeg* succeeds as film at the precise moment the narrator comes to terms with his failure to escape.

# Goat-Glanding and Other Delights: Narration and Sound

I hate the sound of my own voice.

– Guy Maddin[1]

My first contact with Guy Maddin was in 1991. I interviewed him while I was working on the second issue of a zine called *Virus 23*, shortly after he had finished *Archangel*. Even at the time, he already had a well-developed argument about the homogeneity of film sound and his desire to proceed differently:

GUY MADDIN'S RANT ON SOUNDTRACKS

When a painter starts a canvas, he or she can use any kind of brush-stroke desired; they can even throw the paint on with their hands. When a poet puts pen to paper he or she can use any word in the language, or even make one up, but: when a filmmaker adds the soundtrack to his or her movie, it had better be the same kind of soundtrack as all the other movies, or else! Why is it that there is only one kind of movie sound – 'realistic sound' – and that everything that deviates from this is considered 'bad sound'? Why can't sound be slashed and pasted like a crude, but beautiful collage? Why must sounds obey the laws of perspective? I kind of like it when the lips don't quite synch up with the dialogue. It reminds me of when children crayon over the lines in a colouring book. *Why are you people so anal about your children's colouring books?*[2]

In his essay on his collaborations with Guy Maddin, George Toles shows that Maddin's sense of the quality that sound should have in his films, even at this early stage, was as an already mediated memory: 'I recall one of Guy's notes on style for *Archangel*: sound should resemble, *if possible*, an ancient veteran's flickering recollections of his youthful apprenticeship in battlefield atrocities.' These sounds, moreover, should have an uncanny quality: 'a thin, irritating scratching noise persists in this mental fog, as though an unknown animal were clawing against the back door of memory, trying to get in.'[3]

Since that time, Maddin's films have developed as rich and complex a relationship to early aural forms of cinema as they have to its early visual forms. Many of Maddin's films repurpose the various strategies that filmmakers used to construct 'partial talkies' – the first films to feature limited soundtracks in addition to musical accompaniment. Rethinking the history of sound in film for a moment brings about a startling realization: the way that sound works in Maddin's films is more the rule than the exception. Shigehiko Hasumi provocatively points out that, actually, 'the silent film was the typical mode of representation of the 20th century.' Until the late twentieth century, cameras and sound recorders were entirely separate technologies, which could even be said to exist in a relation of mutual exclusivity. This was true until at least 1973, when the Kodak 8mm camera, which could record both sound and video, was released. In other words, most of the 'talking' films that were being made were still really partial talkies. Before fully digital cameras, which could simultaneously record both sound and images on the same media, the notion of 'audiovisuality' itself was a polite fiction.[4] Maddin's films are a reminder of the priority that we still give to the visual over the aural (sound added later can be swapped out entirely, redubbed in ADR, etc.). By evoking the halcyon days of film, they mark the beginning of a true, digital audiovisuality.

Maddin is particularly interested in a hybrid form of partial talkie that involved retroactively adding soundtracks to completed silent films:

> In the months after *The Jazz Singer* was released, it was common to graft primitive soundtracks onto existing movies to bring them up to date with the new technology. This was called 'goat-glanding,' named after a popular medical fad of the day in which monkey and goat glands were transplanted into people apparently without any horrifying rejections or side effects – in an attempt to correct impotence. So it was a way of making movies more potent.[5]

Tim Armstrong maintains that goat-glanding is a useful metaphor for the coming of sound to film, since it both separates and sutures. On the one hand, it begins a recombination of the senses of sight and hearing after their separation in the discrete media forms of the nineteenth century. On the other, the imperfect matching of the moving lips and the emerging voice had something of an uncanny character, as of a voice from beyond the grave,[6] because it poses questions about whose voices an audience is hearing, who controls those voices, and where those voices are coming from. All of these questions are perfectly in keeping with the same sorts of issues that Maddin's overall aesthetic raises.

The subject of narration in Maddin's films requires particular attention, especially since both *My Winnipeg* and its predecessor in the Me Trilogy, *Brand Upon the Brain!* have narrative tracks. Since the 1930s, film theorists such as Paul Rotha have argued that adding sound to films compromised what should have been a purely visual medium in a way that was even 'harmful and detrimental to the public.' Rotha believed that the only exception was the newsreel voiceover. More adventurous filmmakers and film theoreticians, including Eisenstein, viewed sound as one more potentially useful element in montage, as long as it wasn't merely a commercial 'addition.' By and large, though, the critical tendency has been to view narration 'as a threat, as didactic and anti-democratic.'[7] This holds true into the present: for instance, director Ridley Scott first added, then removed, then restored as one option on a deluxe DVD package, Harrison's Ford's voiceover to *Blade Runner*. In one sense, by making narration such an explicit component of his films, Maddin is simply affirming the value of the negative. If, as Richard Drew polemically argued in 1983, 'narration is what you do when you fail,'[8] then narrating an avowed documentary saturated with the failure to leave and forget (his city, his mother) makes perfect sense, but it transforms the failure into a new kind of victory along the way.

Moreover, both *Brand Upon the Brain!* and *My Winnipeg* have been performed in contexts that not only feature narration, but require live narrators. Maddin contextualizes the introduction of narration and other live elements not simply as more than a nuanced stylistic element, but as an actual shift in how he regards his entire project: 'Before I was a filmmaker. Before *Brand Upon the Brain!* But once you start introducing live elements, you really want to make a connection with the audience.'[9] Again, one of the best ways to make something new is to scour the past for unrealized possibilities – ideas that were betrayed by the actual development of events. In many respects, Maddin's desire to position himself as a showman is a return to one of the earliest forms of cinema – what Tom Gunning has famously called 'the cinema of attractions.'[10] One of the key examples Gunning uses is not only one of the earliest films, but also a train film, *The Black Diamond Express* (various versions shot between 1896 and 1903). Albert Smith and John Stuart Blackton, the filmmakers, toured with the film, and Blackton delivered an accompanying lecture to 'startling effect.' The accompanying lecture cuts to the very essence of what made the cinema of attractions powerful. It roots the experience of the film squarely in the present, creating temporal continuity and a feeling of suspense about not *how* the film will unfold, but *when*.[11] Whereas the content of Maddin's films is quite mild compared with what can be found on contemporary cable TV, online, or in the average video rental outlet, the thrill of the physical presence of the director or some other celebrity narrating a film in the same space as an audience is a sensation that filmgoers have not had access to for decades.

Maddin's inspiration for the use of live commentators to accompany his films comes, once again, from the cinema of the 1920s. While reading Luis Buñuel's autobiography *My Last Sigh*, Maddin came across a note mentioning that that 'explicators' often accompanied silent films to explain the new vocabulary of film to audiences. At some point, he also learned about the Benshi, the professional Japanese film commentators from the same period, who sometimes made as much as or more than the actors themselves. Maddin decided to structure *Brand Upon the Brain!* to include such a role, and the film had a wide range of celebrity explicators. The initial run of New York live showings (9–15 May 2007) featured Isabella Rossellini, Lou Reed, Crispin Glover, Laurie Anderson, Justin Bond, Eli Wallach, Anne Jackson, Tunde Adebimpe (of TV on the Radio), Joie Lee, John Ashbery, and Peter Scarlet (of the Tribeca Film Festival) as narrators. All the Chicago shows (18–20 May) featured Crispin Glover's narration. The Los Angeles shows (8–11 June) featured 'scream queen' Barbara Steele, Daniel Handler (author of the Lemony Snicket books), and Udo Kier. The DVD includes a mix of live and studio-recorded narrations by John Ashbery, Crispin Glover, Louis Negin (who also wrote the narration), Isabella Rossellini, Eli Wallach, and Maddin himself.[12] Even though the actual film footage never changes, Maddin observes, it becomes more like theatre because of the variable performance element.[13]

Maddin was pleased enough with the results from the live narration experience with *Brand!* that he resolved to try something similar with *My Winnipeg*. 'The live element,' he says, 'made it more of an event.'[14]

Footage of the Toronto launch for the theatre run of *My Winnipeg* (18 June 2008), with Maddin narrating, appears on the DVD.

A minor counter-tradition in thinking about narration, which goes back as far as the prevailing view, is that narration is always a sort of compromise. Alberto Cavalcanti, for example, laments the tacit restriction of narration to the 'comparatively minor role of providing continuity and "story" in travelogues, newsreels and documentary,'[15] because he was interested in the possibilities of juxtaposing image and sound in order to open up ambiguities rather than fusing them into a harmonious whole. For Bruzzi, narration is not necessarily about consistency and control: 'commentary, far from being a sign of omniscience and control, is the hysterical barrier erected against the spectre of ambivalence and uncertainty.'[16] In other words, narration functions in much the same way as fantasy does. Given that both *Brand Upon the Brain!* and *My Winnipeg* explicitly concern the relation of fantasy to the trauma that it obscures, the choice of adding narration to these films makes good structural sense.

Sound, however, is not the only element that lends an uncanny quality to Maddin's films.

# Viscous and Cottony Hallucinations: Memory and Haunted Media

What's a city without its ghosts?

– Guy Maddin, *My Winnipeg*

'In most of Maddin's films, the past is not exactly recalled,' writes Dennis Lim, 'so much as hallucinated.'[1] One explanation for why this happens so frequently in Maddin's work might be that, as Gilles Deleuze claims, 'Attentive recognition informs us to a much greater degree when it fails than when it succeeds.' When we cannot remember something exactly, what we see in our mind's eye connects to a range of powerful possibilities: déjà vu, dream images, fantasies, scenes recollected from favourite plays, movies and television programs, 'a whole temporal "panorama," an unstable set of floating memories, images of a past *in general* which move past at dizzying speed, as if time were achieving a profound freedom.' The power of these possibilities made them obvious material for the European cinematic tradition of which Maddin is so fond: the Russian constructivists, German Expressionism, and French and Catalonian Surrealism, which collectively developed a panoply of techniques and tropes in order to depict 'amnesia, hypnosis, hallucination, madness, the vision of the dying, and especially nightmare and dream.'[2] Maddin's engagement with these states and the use of the tropes that avant-garde filmmakers developed to depict them are inseparable, which means that the way that his movies depict memory is, literally, *mediated* by the way film historically depicted them.

Our memory is always at least partially the memory of media. Victor Burgin cites a study conducted in 1977 by a sociologist at the University of Provence that lasted a decade and included over 400 oral interviews describing personal memories of 1930–45. 'They found an almost universal tendency for personal history to be mixed with recollections of scenes from films and other media productions. "I saw at the cinema" would become simply "I saw."'[3] Maddin's and Gurdebecke's signature editing style, which they call 'scrolling,' emerges out of just such a fusion of media and memory. This technique, which Maddin is already teaching to students that approach him wishing to learn it, may become one of his lasting contributions to cinematography. In many respects it is the epitome of the contradictions that underpin Maddin's work because, though it somehow evokes the way we imagine silent films to look when skipping and sliding during playback on a rickety old projector, it is possible only because of digital video-editing software.

Maddin offers two parallel origins for the scrolling technique: one in neurophysiological ailments, the other in the practice of using video-editing software. Here is the neurophysiological account:

> I have a neurological ailment that made me think eventually of this style. I have a kind of, this thing, it's very harmless. It's called myoclonus. And I got a cold back in 1989. Some people get them in their sinuses, some in their throat. I got one in the base of my skull. And it created just little neurological flickers that produced tiny little twitches, the kind you just sort of imagine you have most of the time. But just like a ghost touching you with the fingertip. I get them about ten times a minute, just in completely random different places on my body. And I would drive myself nuts thinking a) that I had MS or ALS or something with

initials—'cause the doctors couldn't diagnose it for about a year—but it also just made me very aware of how the nervous system just works in such a scattershot way. And it reminded me of the way memory really does work, too. In movies, when you're presenting memory, you can only ever present a facsimile of memory. Because people don't remember things in chronological order. I just sort of thought that—maybe I'll try presenting, for a change, a different facsimile of memory, using this kind of neurological skittish editing system. There's practical sides to it, too. If a performance ends up being kind of a bit slow, or having some bad stuff in it, you can bite the stuff out or skip it up or speed it up or slow it down – fetishize things. And that, too, is just a facsimile of the way we remember. You know, when you remember – let's say your favorite date ever. Y'know, you're going to skeet, skip ahead quickly to the best part and then go, 'Wait a minute, I've got to back up and slow up into it. And then here it comes again. I'm going too fast.' Back up and then approach it a third time. And then you finally get to the good part, and you slow it up, and suck all of the flavor out of it, and then go skipping off to the next memory, wherever your reveries take you.[4]

Maddin delivers the technical explanation for scrolling in the documentary *97 Percent True*. He and John Gurdebeke developed this technique during the editing of *Cowards Bend the Knee*, with the help of Apple's Final Cut Pro video-editing software. In the digital editing process itself, once fast-forwarding or reversing begins, it is quite easy to move too far past the specific image one is seeking, then too far back, then forward a little slower but still missing the mark, then slightly too far back again, and so on, gradually zeroing in. Maddin compares the effect to skipping a stone over open water. In the technical account of scrolling, he compares this process to memory, but doesn't mention an ailment as its source.

Gurdebecke also notes that, when filming on set, Maddin prefers to shoot very close, so there are always others with cameras on set filming simultaneously to pick up angles that he might miss. The presence of multiple cameras and multiple angles on the same scene lends itself well to the scrolling technique, because there are always other angles to cut into a shot.[5] Again, what we are left with is a standoff between two narratives competing to describe the same phenomena. The solution is not to prioritize one over the other, but to affirm the tension itself as necessary to Maddin's overall aesthetic.

The obverse of memory as mediated is media as memory. Renée Green writes: 'Film is also a memory receptacle: in its most literal sense it is a recorder of light upon emulsion, indexically tracing what was at one time present, to its function as a stimulator of memory associated with the images projected from it.'[6] Because we increasingly remember things in ways that are already mediated, and because media increasingly do much of our remembering for us, many artists have started exploring the relationship between memory and the place that we store our media: the archive.

We believe in the factual efficacy of archives because we believe in the ideology of modern rationalism. If an archive exists, it must consist of documents that were produced objectively, then sorted, catalogued, and stored by professionals thoroughly trained in logical, scientific procedures.[7] And we tend to implicitly treat non-fiction film as a kind of archive of its own because film literally divides the world into uniform chunks and files them in order. However, memory and the archive are not the same thing. In many cases, they end up in direct conflict. Yosef Hayim Yerushalmi writes, 'memory is not an archive, nor is an archive a memory bank. The documents in an archive are not part of memory; if they were, we should have no need to retrieve them; once retrieved, they are often at odds with memory.' Despite the common-sense tendency to think of a film as a sort of archive, the problem is that in any given frame it can create an entirely fabricated document as easily as it can record a legitimate artefact from the past. The results are uncanny, because such films return 'records' that have no real place, collapsing the fantasy of order and rationality upon which the whole notion of the archive is based.[8]

Films like Maddin's push this situation even further by duplicating the look of films that do have some degree of historical authority. Maddin says, 'The 20s just looked cool. They still look cool to this day. It's one of the most durable decades in fashion terms and architectural design terms. There are some others that give it a good run for its money, but it's never gone completely away like some decades do now and then. So I always liked it but I never fell fully in love with 20s cinema until I started making movies myself.'[9] The look that most inspires Maddin's films – the style of the films of the 1920s – comes from films that were being made by people whose entire project, Sven Spieker argues, was to dismantle the faith that nineteenth-century rationality placed in the archive. Through collecting images of 'moments of rupture that elude the archive' and assembling them into films, the artists of the avant-garde strove to point out that 'contingency and chance may affect the archive's operations literally at every level.'[10] Our inability to separate the structure of archival media from the objects that they contain seriously compromises the archive's implicit claims to rationality and objectivity. In an autobiographical film, where the only factor that connects the disparate parts of the film is the bundle of contradictions that is the director, this lack of coherence often becomes even more pronounced.

When discussing the manner in which he deals with historical sources, Maddin places the transfigurative elements of circulation front and centre. He invokes Jorge Luis Borges's story 'Pierre Menard, Author of the *Quixote*,' in which the eponymous Menard does not set out to copy Cervantes's *Don Quixote*, but to produce a number of pages identical to those of Cervantes that are somehow original. In the eyes of the story's narrator, Menard not only succeeds but excels: 'Menard's fragmentary Quixote is more subtle than Cervantes'.'[11] What Maddin tells Michael Ondaatje, though, is, 'I was a really sloppy Menard, which destroys the point of being Menard.' He claims that he can, with full impunity, begin all of his movies as outright plagiarism, knowing he'd ultimately fail to duplicate his source object and would therefore make something new.[12] Harold Bloom calls this initially imperceptible but increasingly rapid departure from the source material one intends to copy 'clinamen,' after the Lucretian term describing the change in movement of atoms that allows anything new to happen in the universe.[13] After an initial attempt at copying, at a certain point the artist swerves from the source. For Bloom, this gesture is both fundamental to the structure of artistic influence and a necessary part of the creative act.

In the specific case of *My Winnipeg*, because Michael Burns had encouraged Maddin from the beginning to think of the film as a personal perspective, he says, 'I no longer felt intimidated by the need to be objective, or even the need to do any research because all the research I needed to do would be, could be done, inside my own heart, or inside my own memories. So everything in the movie is just my feelings about the place. I didn't have to hit the library or the archives or anything like that.'[14] Maddin reiterates this point elsewhere: 'I tried not to do any research. I watched a couple of city documentaries.'[15] The result is a kind of sleepwalking history – a history under the effects of clinamen. The 'otherwise incorruptible' Mayor Cornish ,who presides over the Golden Boy pageant in the film until his era ends in the 1940s, bears little resemblance to Francis Evans Cornish, the first mayor of Winnipeg, who spent one year as mayor in 1874 before he was elected to the Manitoba Legislative Assembly. Cornish, a known drinker, brawler, bigot, as well as a probable bigamist and ballot box stuffer, was anything but incorruptible.[16] The case of the mythical octogenarian hockey team named after the 1929 stock market crash, the Black Tuesdays, who play in the Winnipeg arena even as it is being torn down, is even more vertiginous, because Maddin actually corrects himself after the fact when there was arguably nothing wrong with his continuity to begin with. 'I could have sworn the Crash of 1929 happened on a Tuesday, but nope, it happened on Black Thursday,' Maddin writes.[17] But 29 October 1929 *was* a Tuesday. The slide of the market began five days earlier, on a Thursday, but the expression 'Black Tuesday' has been in the popular vernacular for decades. Chasing down such errors is amusing in a pedantic sort of way, but ultimately is pointless. The most sage perspective on the subject of Maddin's historical continuity actually comes from Borges's narrator again: 'Historical truth, for Menard, is not "what happened"; it is what we *believe* happened.' The practice of 'deliberate anachronism and fallacious attribution,' he concludes, 'fills the calmest book with adventure.'[18] Similarly, even Winnipeg's Garbage Hill, the most random and mundane of archives, becomes thrilling and dangerous. Jagged objects heave from beneath the frozen ground to snag unwary sledders, just as objects emerge from the archive to snag the director's interest … or bizarre fragments of the film suddenly seize the attention of the unwary viewer like an apparition from beyond the grave.

Guy Maddin was seven years old when his older brother Cameron died. That same day, Guy received Cameron's room, his vacuum-tube radio, and his reel-to-reel tape recorder. Around 2005, Maddin came across a collection of tapes that his brother had made as a boy, and he went through an elaborate, irreversible process to have them digitized (the lab that digitized the tapes flash-heated them to prevent them from snapping while playing them back in order to re-record them, which renders the originals unusable immediately afterward). What Maddin found was a form of sound sculpture, an audio palimpsest that forms the perfect complement to the visual palimpsest of the Forks, his mother's lap, the railways, and the alleyways:

I discovered that he was making these recordings of these same acoustic landscapes. Trying to find little stations talking about interesting things of 1959 or 1961 – Marilyn Monroe's suicide or American Air Force talk radio from 1961 of UFO sightings and conspiracy theories. Not much different from late-night talk radio now, but sounding so much better because it was filtered through all sorts of distant crackles. Every now and then you'd find out that something was originating from Houston or something like that. It created a world.[19]

Excerpts of Cameron Maddin's recordings form the soundtrack that accompanies the section of the film about Winnipeg's 'illicit' and 'shameful' back alleys: 'In the alleyways, strange wavelengths predominate,' says the narration. In his annotations to the script, Maddin describes these recordings as 'dreamy and terrifying.'[20] In a word, haunted. As the director is haunted by his media, the film is haunted by these recordings.

Like all of the other forms of electromechanical media that came into existence in the second half of the nineteenth century, radio has always been haunted. As Jeffrey Sconce describes in *Haunted Media*, during the same period, thanks to the enthusiasms of Kate and Margaret Fox of Hydesville, New York, the practice of attempting to communicate with the spirits of the dead became a continent-wide craze.[21] The logical question to ask of each new communications medium that came along was if, along with its other startlingly novel and powerful attributes, it might also permit communication with the dead. John Durham Peters notes that the inception of organized spiritualism happened very quickly after cities began to be linked by the telegraph, and that spiritualism 'explicitly modeled itself of the telegraph's ability to receive remote messages.' That both spiritualism and electromechanical communications use the term 'medium' to describe the device that conveys messages demonstrates the inseparability at the very level of language of these two fields. For Peters, 'all mediated communication is in a sense communication with the dead, insofar as media can store "phantasms of the living" for playback after bodily death.'[22] It is almost unremarkable, then, that the narrator of *My Winnipeg* relates to Winnipeg history largely through haunted media. He imagines using Cameron's huge, obsolete radio to listen to two of Winnipeg's late radio celebrities, Kenny 'Friar' Nicholson and 'Cactus' Jack Wells, do the play-by-play for the ghostly Black Tuesdays in the haunted arena, but who else would do it?[23] 'How can one live without his ghosts?' is a rhetorical question.

The archive, it seems, is also haunted. It holds the potential to confound, complicate, and confuse official accounts of history as well as to provide accurate witnessing.[24] For example, consider the Hamilton Family Fonds in the Archives & Special Collections of the University of Manitoba Libraries.[25] Dr Thomas Glendenning Hamilton was a prominent Winnipeg physician, a long-term MLA, and a practising spiritualist after losing his son in World War I. Between 1918 and 1945, he and his wife Lillian Hamilton conducted regular séances in their home – and, apparently, in the cottage seven doors down from the Maddins at Loni Beach in Gimli, something Maddin learned of only recently.[26] The Hamiltons left an extensive collection of books, devices, slides from lectures, notes, and photographs to the university, which has digitized hundreds of images detailing 'numerous aspects of spiritualism including telekinesis, teleplasm, trance states and various other psychic phenomena.'[27] These images put some interesting kinks in the standard notion that archival footage is somehow 'true' because it's old. Obviously faked photos of cotton-batting ectoplasm coming out of a person's nose might not tell us more in the end than the séance scene in *My Winnipeg*.

Which is a long way from saying that they tell us nothing at all. Spiritualist media artefacts such as photos and recordings convey reams of historically specific information about the technologies that people thought appropriate to visualize the immaterial. They provide some historical context for the digital media ghosts of *Poltergeist* (1982), *Ringu* (1992), and the various sequels, remakes, and imitations that comprise today's haunted media landscape, which no longer look quite so odd by comparison. They also convey the constantly foiled but unreasonable hope that most people bear in their hearts that communication could ever be something other than the risk of total loss of meaning. When the dead communicate via their stored impressions, as on Cameron Maddin's reel-to-reel tapes, communication takes places as a one-way process. Accordingly, the medium or in this case, Maddin as the writer, needs to conduct both sides of the discussion. As John Durham Peters observes, this isn't as counterproductive as it might first seem: 'It would be foolish to disparage communications that never leave our own circle as only failures. Perhaps all dialogue involves each partner's enacting the response of the other. Dialogic ideology keeps us from seeing that expressive acts occurring over distances and without immediate assurance of reply can be desperate and daring acts of dignity.'[28] *My Winnipeg* accords that degree of risk and dignity to the ghost of Cameron Maddin. Desperate and daring as it might be, the question that arises is how dignified is the séance in the film that occurs before the grand staircase of the Manitoba Legislative building.

In *My Winnipeg*, spiritualism is a strategy for addressing blockages in circulation. Lou Profeta's exorcism of a baulky streetcar, though, is a synecdoche for a larger problem. In Maddin's film, Winnipeg is a city constituted around a gap. It is not only a city with no founding legends, but a city whose downtown had literally been gutted, first by the saturation of mall space in the 1980s that wiped out street-level pedestrian traffic, then by the removal of historic buildings as the businesses they once contained went bankrupt when the downtown lost customers to big-box retail on the city's edges. The narration of *My Winnipeg* contains nothing but scorn for the MTS Centre, the downtown arena erected in the space that once contained the Eaton's department store, referring to it as the 'Empty Centre,' as the image of the neon sign's 'S' flickers dimly onscreen, reducing the logo to its first two letters. Around this very Real gap, a trauma that threatens to destroy the city (demolition being one of its only growth industries, deadpans the narrator), rages the city's constantly waged war between two worlds. One world, the Symbolic/believable, is the one in which Winnipeggers live now. The other is the one they expect to inhabit in the future – the Imaginary/memorable. The film's séance, whose guests include not only the mayor and other city officials, but also Winnipeg's prostitutes and other denizens of the labyrinthine aspect of the city, becomes a kind of spiritual parliament that doubles the Legislative Assembly, attempting to negotiate for one world for both the spiritual and the physical inhabitants of the province.

The séance scene itself is one of the moments in *My Winnipeg* that comes closest to the melodrama of Maddin's fictional, partial-talkie films shot in black and white, especially *Archangel*, *Cowards Bend the Knee*, and *Brand Upon the Brain!*. Since it incorporates dance and features RWB corps de ballet member Jacelyn Lobay playing Gweneth Lloyd (co-founder of the Royal Winnipeg Ballet) as a medium, we could also add *Dracula – Pages from a Virgin's Diary* to this list. Maddin's own comments about melodrama as psychological truth already suggest that we might think about this scene as more than kitsch and hysteria, but he has also filmed it in a way that lends a certain dignity to the proceedings that the montage of the Hamilton photos lacks – moving, perhaps, even into the logic of opera. When Eric Nipp, as the young Viscount Gort, is possessed by the spirit of Hermes, he appears not as the Golden Boy overhead but in his aspect as a wounded god, paradoxically both immortal and dying. Alone, he is castrated and weak, but with the support of Lloyd, possessed by the spirit of Otter Heart the Raft Girl, they begin

Althea Cornish in a trance. Courtesy of Guy Maddin, from the director's personal collection.

a duet that will ford them across the Forks. This dance transforms the nature of Hermes' relation to his wound. Otter Heart is the fantasy that supports him and the unsustainable dream of getting over the Forks, out of Winnipeg and the impossible sublimity at its heart. Like all attempts to escape, this one is thwarted by the intervention of Althea Cornish, the mayor's daughter, who is possessed by Es-tonea-pesla, Cree Princess of the Cold. Here, as elsewhere in the film, cold is the Real that blocks all passage. Hermes embraces the Cold Princess, who imprisons Otter Heart, then swoons. The spiritualists awake from their trance and gather uncertainly around Althea's prone form. Cut to white, blowing snow against a black background: the Real of televisual static and the Real of the weather.

The question is this: is Hermes' embracing of the Princess of the Cold actually the correct decision rather than a betrayal? When psychoanalysis insists that the key to traversing the fantasy is 'not to give way to one's desire,' Slavoj Žižek argues, 'the desire with regard to which we must not "give way" is not the desire supported by fantasy but the desire of the Other beyond fantasy. "Not to give way on desire" implies a radical renunciation of all the richness of desires based upon fantasy-scenarios.'[29] In such a scenario, where the cold, empty heart of Winnipeg is accepted for what it is, as in Wagnerian opera, 'what appears as "wound" is actually a positive condition of "healing": the inaccessibility of the Thing is a positive condition of our freedom and moral dignity.'[30] The most melodramatic scene in the film, then, holds the key to the questions posed by its most straightforward, documentary aspects.

*My Winnipeg* is in many respects an artefact of the director's attempts to remember the changing conditions of media over his lifetime. Digitization changes the entire cultural order, transforming the most ephemeral and obscure documents, like the Hamilton photos, into material that can be located instantly via Web search. Renée Green writes, 'As the technology of film has shifted the mourning of different film eras has ensued, as well as an increased amount of language produced about film.'[31] One of the most dignified possible responses is to transform the mourning into art.

# Beautifully Broken: Conclusions

Ever tried. Ever failed. No matter. Try again. Fail again. Fail better.

– Samuel Beckett, *Worstward Ho*

'Archives do not record experience so much as its absence,' writes Sven Spieker. 'They mark the point where an experience is missing from its proper place, and what is returned to us in an archive may well be something we never possessed in the first place.'[1] In recording his attempt to restore the things that were missing from his sense of what constitutes his life in Winnipeg, the things that haunt him about it, what Maddin has created is not a verisimilitude, but something else entirely.

Ty Burr pinpoints the issue: the underlying message of *My Winnipeg* is that 'modernity is a broken thing.'[2] If city symphonies by the likes of Ruttmann and Vertov constructed a kind of visual plenitude, a hymn to the fragmented splendours of mechanized modernity that was paid for with the cost of the classical notion of human subjectivity,[3] in *My Winnipeg*, Maddin is telling the story of a city that is already castrated by its frozen racehorses, displaced hockey team, and demolished buildings, all of its early promise long since vanished under a tawdry and barely cohesive retrofit. He re-images the genre to tell the story of the modern city's end rather than its beginning.

*My Winnipeg* appears at a historical moment when both the modernist dream of 'the city' and 'cinema' as a historically specific structure of visibility are slipping away.[4] The way we think of spatial organization now has more to do with the way that TV, video and the Internet inscribe it than the way that film does. Maddin's response, beginning with *Brand Upon the Brain!*, has been to change the boundaries of what constitutes a film in order to keep pace, experimenting with live performers, the full range of options that DVD has to offer, new distribution channels like YouTube, and the still-rich possibilities of the book, joking that now that he has published memoirs, film treatments, annotated scripts, the collages he has used as storyboards, and an annotated script, the next step might be to attempt to recuperate that most loathed of all literary forms, the film novelization.[5] An upcoming Internet-based collaboration with American poet John Ashbery, if it occurs, will make the assemblage of Maddin's differential 'filmography' all the more complex. Maddin's now-standard interview line 'before [*Brand!*] I was a filmmaker' is a recognition that what it means to make a movie is changing, and that calling oneself a filmmaker in such a milieu might soon be the equivalent of referring to a car as a 'horseless carriage.' The ghost of Marshall McLuhan would approve.

In *My Winnipeg*, Guy Maddin attempts something difficult: dramatizing the shift of desire into drive, which is possible only when the fantasy of escape – which is always a particular kind of failure – is abandoned. Endlessly circling around the gaping absence at the heart of his gutted city, the flattened arena, and his empty beauty-parlor home, he embraces the Cold and imagines himself building a rooftop Happyland out of rubble. Presiding over it all is his Marxist 'page 3' girl, Citizen Girl. Like 'Anna, Scientist' from *Heart of the World*, she is part Oktobriana-style superhero and part communist media muse (Maddin professes to being an 'old Communist' at heart[6]), constituted by the newspaper as the embodiment of the citizenry themselves. Like all utopian fantasies, this one is impossible and it too will crumble. When it does, the markers

Citizen Girl and the old Clifford's sign. Courtesy of Guy Maddin, from the director's personal collection.

on the border between the thinkable and the unthinkable will have shifted a little further out.

One way to assess both *My Winnipeg* and the trajectory of Maddin's larger project would be to return to one of my starting points: Raymond Williams's dialectic of the residual, the dominant, and the emergent. By repurposing the half-forgotten residual forms of 1920s film for his own purposes, Maddin attempts to fashion an emergent cinema that requires his audiences to consider the contexts through which his film circulates, and how that process of circulation transfigures the 'film' itself. As Williams points out, 'it is never a matter of immediate practice; indeed it depends crucially on finding new forms or adaptations of form. Again and again what we have to observe is in effect a *pre-emergence*, active and pressing but not yet fully articulated, rather than the evident emergence which could be more confidently named.'[7] In these terms Maddin's films, especially *My Winnipeg*, constitute the pre-emergence of a differential digital cinema that embodies a potentially resistant set of cultural practices. Here, as elsewhere, emergence is an ongoing process. History is a beginning, not an end.[8]

# Production Credits

**Production Company**
IFC Films

**Director**
Guy Maddin

**Writers**
Guy Maddin
George Toles (dialogue writer)

**Cast**
(all significant speaking roles)

| | |
|---|---|
| Ann Savage | Mother |
| Louis Negin | Mayor Cornish |
| Amy Stewart | Janet Maddin |
| Darcy Fehr | Ledgeman; Sleeper on train ('Guy Maddin'?) |
| Brendan Cade | Cameron Maddin |
| Wesley Cade | Ross Maddin |
| Lou Profeta | Himself |
| Fred Dunsmore: | Himself |
| Kate Yacula | Citizen Girl |
| Jacelyn Lobay | Gweneth Lloyd |
| Eric Nipp | Viscount Gort |

Jennifer Palichuk      Althea Cornish
Deborah Carlson
Kevin Harris
Scott Hamel
Wayne Hamel
Olie Alto
Jeremy Dangerfield
Daniel Hussey
Tim Kiriluk
Lee Major
Roy Trumpour
Chris Turyk
John Warkentin
Will Woytowich      Con Johanesson
Brett Donahue
Guy Maddin      Narrator
(non-speaking roles)
Kalyn Bomback      Sleepwalker
Cory Cassidy      Russian Bolshevik
Aaron Hughes      If Day Nazi
Joyce Krenz      Auntie
Mel Marginet      Paddlewheel Woman
Bronwyn Ring      Girl At The Paddlewheel (uncredited)

**Producers**
Michael Burns (executive producer)
Phyllis Laing
Guy Maddin
Jody Shapiro

**Original Music**
Jason Staczek

**Cinematographer**
Jody Shapiro

**Film Editor**
John Gurdebeke

**Casting**
Jim Heber
Patricia Kress (extras)

**Production Design**
Réjean Labrie

**Art Direction**
Katharina Stieffenhofer

**Set Decoration**
Chad Giesbrecht
John Jennissen
Alexis Labra
Bill MacInnis

**Costume Design**
Meg McMillan

**Makeup**
Ediena Hawkes (key hair stylist)
Brianne Lewin (key makeup artist)

**Assistant Director** (second unit director)
Richard Duffy (second assistant director)
Danielle Dumesnil (first assistant director)
Leona Krahn (third assistant director)
Ronaldo Nacionales (first assistant director)
Lori Stefaniuk (second assistant director)

**Sound Department**

Michel Germain (voiceover recording engineer)

Martin Lee (sound re-recording mixer)

Cameron Maddin (sound sculpture)

David McCallum (sound)

Steve Medeiros (sound editor)

Joe Morrow (sound re-recording assistant)

Jordan Pede (boom operator)

Marvin Polanski (production sound mixer)

David Rose (sound)

Jane Tattersall (sound editor)

**Visual Effects**

Tim J. Langevin (visual effects assistant)

**Running Time**

80 minutes

**Aspect Ratio**

1.33:1

# Further Viewing

**Cowards Bend the Knee** (or **The Blue Hands**). Guy Maddin. 2003
**Brand upon the Brain!** Guy Maddin. The Film Company. 2006

# Notes

## 1. Breaking and Entering: An Introduction

1 Ondaatje, 'Guy Maddin and Michael Ondaatje,' 134.
2 Maddin, 'My Winnipeg,' 25.
3 Vatnsdal, *Kino Delirium*, 10.
4 Miller, 'Cinema Studies Doesn't Matter,' 306.
5 Burgin, *In/Different Spaces*, 22–3.
6 Darr, 'Haunted Childhood.'
7 Burgin, *Remembered Film*, 9–10.
8 Vatnsdal, *Kino Delirium*, 25.
9 Maddin, *From the Atelier*, 176, 91.
10 Ibid., 191.
11 Maddin, 'Personal Interview,'
12 Burgin, *Remembered Film*, 10.
13 Alifragkis and Penz, 'Spatial Dialectics,' 222.
14 Higgins and Higgins, 'Intermedia.'
15 Youngblood, *Expanded Cinema*, 54.
16 Jenkins, 'Transmedia Storytelling.'
17 Perloff, '"Vocable Scriptsigns,"' 101.
18 Maddin, 'My Winnipeg,' 40.
19 Williams, *Marxism and Literature*, 122, 123.
20 Acland, *Residual Media*, xxi, xx.
21 Williams, *Marxism and Literature*, 125.
22 Acland, *Residual Media*, xvi.

23 Straw, 'Reinhabiting Lost Languages,' 306–7.

24 Vatnsdal, *Kino Delirium*, 80.

25 Shaviro, 'Fire and Ice,' 216.

26 Straw, 'Reinhabiting Lost Languages,' 310.

27 Scott, 'Permafrost.'

28 Darr, 'Haunted Childhood.'

29 Gaonkar and Povinelli, Technologies of Public Forms,' 386.

30 Straw, 'Circulatory Turn,' 9, 14.

31 Žižek, *Plague of Fantasies*, 10.

32 Žižek, *For They Know Not*, 272.

## 2. Transfusions: Biography and Filmography

1 Maddin, 'Annotated Script,' 174.

2 Halfyard, 'Guy Maddin Talks'; ibid.

3 Halfyard, 'Guy Maddin Talks.'

4 Maddin, 'Annotated Script,' 36.

5 Canadian Press, 'Manitoba Set for TV Debut.'

6 Maddin, 'Annotated Script,' 36.

7 Žižek, *Enjoy Your Symptom!*, 126, 133.

8 Vatnsdal, *Kino Delirium*, 27.

9 Maddin, 'Annotated Script.'

10 Maddin, *Atelier Tovar*, 178.

11 Peters, *Speaking into the Air*, 153.

12 Darr, Haunted Childhood.

13 Douglas, *Listening In*, 72–7.

14 Ondaatje, 'Guy Maddin and Michael Ondaatje, ' 149.

15 Wershler-Henry, 'Strangled by an Intestine!,' 13.

16 Maddin, 30 June 2009.

17 Canavese, 'Guy Maddin.'

18 Austin-Smith, 'Strange Frontiers,' 243–4.

19 Vatnsdal, *Kino Delirium*, 55.

20 McCaffery and nichol, *Rational Geomancy*, 12–13.

21 Vatnsdal, *Kino Delirium*, 127.

22 Wershler-Henry, 'Strangled by an Intestine!,' 14.

23 Ebert, '*My Winnipeg*,' 381.

24 Žižek, *Organs without Bodies*, 12.

25 Green, 'Survival,' 54.

26 Ondaatje, 'Guy Maddin and Michael Ondaatje,' 140–1.

27 Vatnsdal, *Kino Delirium*, 29–36.

28 Ibid., 55–6.

29 Ondaatje, 'Guy Maddin and Michael Ondaatje,' 132.

30 Vatnsdal, *Kino Delirium*, 47.

31 Ibid., 62.

32 Maddin, 'Personal Interview.'

33 Wershler-Henry, 'Strangled by an Intestine!,' 12.

34 Vatnsdal, *Kino Delirium*, 90.

35 Maddin, 'Personal Interview.'

36 Vatnsdal, *Kino Delirium*, 97–9.

37 Toles and Maddin, 'Dikemaster's Daughter.'

38 Vatnsdal, *Kino Delirium*, 112, 15.

39 Vatnsdal, 'Strange Direction,' 184.

40 Ondaatje, 'Guy Maddin and Michael Ondaatje,' 144, 145.

41 Diones, 'Dracula.'

42 Ibid.

43 Maddin, *Cowards Bend the Knee*, 14.

44 Seitz, 'Funny Guy.'

45 Corliss, 'Heady Brew.'

46 Ibid.

47 McBride, 'Brain Storm.'

48 Jameson, 'Utopia and Failure.'

49 *97 Percent True.*

50 Straw, 'Reinhabiting Lost Languages,' 311.

51 *97 Percent True.*

52 Seguin, 'Winnipeg, Mon Amour.'

53 'Film Critic Top Ten.'

54 Ebert, 'The Best Films.'

55 Seguin, 'Winnipeg, Mon Amour.'

56 Morgenstern, "Kit Kittredge,'

57 Hoberman, 'Werner Herzog and Guy Maddin.'

58  Kennicott, 'It's Tough to Escape.'
59  AlSayyad, *Cinematic Urbanism*, 34.

## 3. The Peculiar Enchantments of Winnipeg: The Commission

1  'Soda Pictures Theatrical Press Kit, 5.'
2  Maddin, 'Personal Interview.'
3  Rossellini, *In the Name of the Father*
4  Maddin, 'Personal Interview.'
5  Ibid.
6  Wigon, 'Tribeca Film Festival 2008.'
7  'Soda Pictures Theatrical Press Kit.'
8  Douglas, 'Exclusive.'
9  Wigon, 'Tribeca Film Festival 2008.'
10  Seguin, 'Winnipeg, Mon Amour.'
11  Ondaatje, 'Guy Maddin and Michael Ondaatje,' 130.
12  Wigon, 'Tribeca Film Festival 2008.'
13  Leone, 'Textual Wanderings,' 90, 90–1.
14  Maddin, 'Annotated Script,' 116.
15  Certeau, 'Walking in the City,' 106, 107.
16  Maddin, 'Annotated Script,' 40.
17  Nadeau, 'Interview with Guy Maddin.'
18  Ondaatje, 'Guy Maddin and Michael Ondaatje,' 137.
19  Maddin, 'Personal Interview.'
20  Maddin, 'Annotated Script,' 13.
21  Nadeau, 'Interview with Guy Maddin.'
22  Darr, 'Haunted Childhood.'
23  Prigge, 'Dizzy Rascal.'
24  Enright, 'Chicken Soup,' 144.
25  Maddin, 'Personal Interview.'
26  Maddin, 'Annotated Script,' 30.
27  Edroso, 'Ann Savage.'
28  mabnyc, 'Ann Savage 1921–2008.'
29  Maddin, 'Personal Interview.'
30  Maddin, 'Annotated Script.'

31  Maddin, 'Personal Interview.'
32  Wigon, 'Tribeca Film Festival 20008.'
33  Nadeau, 'Interview with Guy Maddin.'
34  Ibid.
35  Halfyard, 'Guy Maddin Talks.'
36  Darr, 'Haunted Childhood.'
37  Newman, 'February 19, 1942: If Day.'
38  Smetanka, 'Cold Throbbings,' 172.
39  Maddin, 'Personal Interview.'
40  Maddin, 'Annotated Script.'
41  Ibid., 34.
42  Nichols, *Representing Reality*, 160–1.
43  Bruzzi, *New Documentary*, 26.

## 4. A Glorious Dress-up Chest: Genre

1  Beard, 'Guy Maddin and Cinematography,' 31.
2  Woloski, 'Guy Maddin.'
3  Halfyard, 'Guy Maddin Talks.'
4  Bakhtin, *Problems of Dostoevsky's Poetics*, 18.
5  Wigon, 'Tribeca Film Festival, 2008.'
6  Ondaatje, 'Guy Maddin and Michael Ondaatje,' 133.
7  Seitz, 'Funny Guy.'
8  Beard, 'Madden and Melodrama,' 12.
9  Nichols, *Blurred Boundaries*, 1.
10  Bruzzi, *New Documentary*, 13.
11  E. Douglas, 'Exclusive.'
12  Natter, 'The City as Cinematic Space,' 213–14.
13  Maddin, 'Personal Interview.'
14  Beard, 'Madden and Melodrama,' 12, 11–12.
15  Žižek, *Enjoy Your Symptom!*, 123.
16  Beard, 'Maddin and Melodrama,' 13.
17  Žižek, *Enjoy Your Symptom!*, 120.
18  Ibid., 123.
19  Žižek, *The Parallax View*, 123.

20  Maddin, 'Annotated Script,' 36.
21  Žižek, *For They Know Not*, 10–11.
22  Bruzzi, *New Documentary*, 43, 46.
23  Stone quoted in ibid., 44.
24  Nichols, '"Getting to Know You,"' 176, 177.
25  Ondaatje, 'Guy Maddin and Michael Ondaatje,' 138.
26  Maddin, 'Annotated Script,' 98, 97.
27  Smetanka, 'Cold Throbbings,' 172.
28  Deleuze, *Cinema 2*, 152–3.

## 5.  More Ellipses: The City and Circulation

 1  L'Atelier National du Manitoba, 'Tragedy of the Winnipeg Jets.'
 2  Pound, 'Paris Letter.'
 3  Williams, *The Country and the City*, 290–1.
 4  Pinkney, 'Editor's Introduction,' 11.
 5  Donald, 'The City, the Cinema,' 912.
 6  Certeau, "Walking in the City,' 94, 92.
 7  MacDonald, "The City as Motion Picture,' 111.
 8  Barber, *Projected Cities*, 24, 20,
 9  Ibid., 17–18.
10  Certeau, 'Walking in the City,' 92, 92–3.
11  Dolar, 'I Shall Be with You,' 7.
12  Donald, 'The City, the Cinema,' 78.
13  Certeau, 'Walking in the City,' 95, 105.
14  Žižek, *Tarrying with the Negative*, 90.
15  Strathausen, 'Uncanny Spaces,' 17.
16  Donald, 'The City, the Cinema,' 88.
17  MacDonald, 'The City as Motion Picture,' 111–12.
18  Kracauer, *From Caligari to Hitler*, 181, 184.
19  MacDonald, 'The City as Motion Picture,' 112.
20  Donald, 'The City, the Cinema,' 84–5.
21  Bruzzi, *New Documentary*, 84.
22  Strathausen, 'Uncanny Spaces,' 27.
23  Donald, 'The City, the Cinema,' 79–80.

24  Ibid., 87.

25  Alifragkis and Penz, 'Spatial Dialectics,' 222, 223.

26  Donald, 'The City, the Cinema,' 86.

27  Kracauer, *From Caligari to Hitler*, 185–6.

28  Seguin, 'Winnipeg, Mon Amour.'

29  Kitchener-Waterloo Art Gallery, 'Online Exhibitions.'

30  Hoberman, 'Werner Herzog and Guy Maddin.'

31  Donald, 'The City, the Cinema,' 88.

32  Certeau, 'Walking in the City,' 107.

33  Maddin, 'Personal Interview.'

34  Maddin, 'Annotated Script,' 173.

35  Natter, 'The City as Cinematic Space,' 217, 218.

36  Maddin, 'Annotated Script,' 12.

37  Barber, *Projected Cities*, 32.

38  Schivelbusch, *The Railway Journey*, 61.

39  Deleuze, *Cinema 2*, 36–7.

40  Ibid.

41  Maddin, 'Personal Interview.'

42  Maddin, 'Annotated Script,' 13.

43  Seguin, 'Winnipeg, Mon Amour.'

44  Wigon, 'Tribeca Film Festival 2008.'

## 6.  The Forks beneath the Forks: Desire and Drive

1  Vatnsdal, *Kino Delirium*, 90.

2  Darrell Varga, 'Desire in Bondage,' 59.

3  Žižek, *On Belief* , 94–5.

4  Babuscio, 'Camp and the Gay Sensibility,' 20.

5  Sullivan, *Queer Theory*, vi.

6  O'Donoghue, 'Particles of Illusion.'

7  Meyer, 'Discourse of Camp,' 137.

8  Sedgwick, *Between Men*, 1–2.

9  Vatnsdal, *Kino Delirium*, 30.

10  Ibid., 91.

11  Ibid., 30.

12  Peters, *Speaking into the Air*, 50.

13  Kroetsch, *Lovely Treachery of Words*, 18.

14  Maddin, *Atelier Tovar*, 80–3.

15  Maddin, 'Annotated Script,' 10.

16  Maddin, 'Personal Interview.'

17  Wershler-Henry, 'Return from Without,' 318, 24–5.

18  Goldie, *Fear and Temptation*.

19  Bey, *Taz*.

20  Maddin, 'Personal Interview.'

21  Maddin, *Atelier Tovar*, 55–6.

22  Beard, 'Conversations with Guy Maddin,' 14.

23  Maddin, 'Annotated Script,' 11.

24  Maddin, 'Personal Interview.'

25  Varga, 'Desire in Bondage,' 62.

26  Vatnsdal, *Kino Delirium*, 101.

27  Žižek, *Sublime Object of Ideology*, 118.

28  Maddin, 'Annotated Script,' 31.

29  Žižek, *Plague of Fantasies*, 31.

30  Žižek, *On Belief*, 96.

## 7.  Goat-Glanding and Other Delights: Narration and Sound

1  Maddin, 'Personal Interview.'

2  Wershler-Henry, 'Strangled by an Intestine!,' 13.

3  Toles, 'From Archangel to Mandragora,' 325.

4  Hasumi, 'Fiction and the "Unrepresentable,"' 327, 320.

5  Vatnsdal, *Kino Delirium*, 64.

6  Armstrong, *Modernism, Technology, and the Body*, 226, 223–4.

7  Rotha quoted in Bruzzi, *New Documentary*, 47, 48.

8  Drew quoted in ibid.

9  Canavese, 'Guy Maddin,'

10  Gunning, 'An Aesthetic of Astonishment,' 116.

11  Gunning, '"Now You See It,"' 7.

12  '*Brand Upon the Brain!* Presskit.'

13  *97 Percent True*.

14 Halfyard, 'Guy Maddin Talks.'
15 Cavalcanti, quoted in Bruzzi, *New Documentary*, 58.
16 Bruzzi in ibid.

## 8. Viscous and Cottony Hallucinations: Memory and Haunted Media

1 Lim, 'Out of the Past,' 5.
2 Deleuze, *Cinema 2*, 54–5, 55.
3 Burgin, *Remembered Film*, 68.
4 Canavese, 'Guy Maddin.'
5 *97 Percent True.*
6 Green, 'Survival,' 53.
7 Spieker, *The Big Archive*, 6.
8 Yerushalmi in ibid., 4.
9 Darr, 'Haunted Childhood.'
10 Spieker, *The Big Archive*, 6–7.
11 Borges, 'Pierre Menard,' 93.
12 Ondaatje, 'Guy Maddin and Michael Ondaatje,' 139, 132.
13 Bloom, *The Anxiety of Influence*, 14, 19–45.
14 Wigon, 'Tribeca Film Festival 2008.'
15 Halfyard, 'Guy Maddin Talks.'
16 Bloom, *The Anxiety of Influence*.
17 Maddin, 'Annotated Script,' 91.
18 Borges, 'Pierre Menard,' 94, 95.
19 Darr, 'Haunted Childhood.'
20 Maddin, 'Annotated Script,' 77.
21 Sconce, *Haunted Media*, 22–4.
22 Peters, *Speaking into the Air*, 94–5, 142.
23 Maddin, 'Annotated Script,' 93.
24 Merewether, 'Art and the Archive,' 11.
25 Archives & Special Collections, 'Hamilton Family Fonds.'
26 Maddin, 'Annotated Script,' 63.
27 Archives & Special Collections, 'Hamilton Family Fonds.'
28 Peters, *Speaking into the Air*, 152.
29 Žižek, *Sublime Object*, 118.

30  Žižek, *Tarrying with the Negative*, 194.
31  Green, 'Survival,' 53.

## 9. Beautifully Broken: Conclusions

1  Spieker, *The Big Archive*, 3.
2  Burr, 'Funky, Funny "Winnipeg."'
3  Strathausen, 'Uncanny Spaces,' 29.
4  Donald, 'The City, the Cinema,' 93.
5  Maddin, 'Personal Interview.'
6  Ibid.
7  Williams, *Marxism and Literature*, 126.
8  Deleuze, *Cinema 2*, 96–7.

# Bibliography

Acland, Charles R., ed. *Residual Media*. Minneapolis: University of Minnesota Press, 2007.

Alifragkis, Stavros, and François Penz. 'Spatial Dialectics: Montage and Spatially Organised Narrative in Stories without Human Leads.' *Digital Creativity* 17: 4 (2006): 221–33.

AlSayyad, Nezar. *Cinematic Urbanism: A History of the Modern from Real to Reel*. New York/London: Routledge, 2006.

Archives & Special Collections. 'Hamilton Family Fonds.' University of Manitoba Libraries.

Armstrong, Tim. *Modernism, Technology, and the Body: A Cultural Study*. New York: Cambridge University Press, 1998.

Austin-Smith, Brenda. 'Strange Frontiers: Twenty Years of Manitoba Feature Film.' In *Self Portraits: The Cinemas of Canada since Telefilm*, ed. André Loiselle and Tom McSorley. 237–70. Ottawa: The Canadian Film Institute, 2006.

Babuscio, Jack. 'Camp and the Gay Sensibility.' In *Camp Grounds: Style and Homosexuality*, ed. David Bergman. 19–38. Amherst: University of Massachusetts Press, 1993.

Bakhtin, Mikhail. *Problems of Dostoevsky's Poetics*. Edited by Wlad Godzich and Jochen Schulte-Sasse. Theory and History of Literature. Minneapolis: University of Minnesota Press, 1984.

Barber, Stephen. *Projected Cities*. London: Reaktion Books, 2002.

Beard, William. 'Conversations with Guy Maddin.' Edited by Metro Cinema Society. Edmonton: Metro Cinema Publications, 2007.

– 'Guy Maddin and Cinematography: An Interview.' *Cinephile* 5: 1 (2009): 29–36.

– 'Maddin and Melodrama.' 14: 2 (2005): 217.

Benjamin, Walter. '*Berlin Chronicle.*' In *Walter Benjamin: Selected Writings*, ed. Michael W. Jennings, Howard Eiland, and Gary Smith 595–637. Cambridge, Mass./London: Belknap Press of Harvard University Press, 2005.

Bey, Hakim. *TAZ: The Temporary Autonomous Zone, Ontological Anarchy, Poetic Terrorism.* 3rd ed. New Autonomy Series. Brooklyn, N.Y.: Autonomedia, 2003.

Bloom, Harold. *The Anxiety of Influence: A Theory of Poetry.* New York: Oxford University Press, 1973.

Borges, Jorge Luis. 'Pierre Menard, Author of the Quixote.' In *Collected Fictions.* 88-95. New York: Viking, 1998.

'*Brand Upon the Brain!* Presskit.' American Cinematheque. http://www.american-cinematheque.com/archive1999/BrandupontheBrain/BrandContents.html.

Bruzzi, Stella. *New Documentary.* 2nd ed. Abingdon: Routledge, 2006.

Burgin, Victor. *In/Different Spaces: Place and Memory in Visual Culture.* Berkeley: University of California Press, 1996.

– *The Remembered Film.* London: Reaktion, 2004.

Burr, Ty. 'His Is a Funky, Funny "Winnipeg."' *Boston Globe.* http://www.boston.com/movies/display?display=movie&id=11495.

Canadian Press. 'Manitoba Set for TV Debut on CBC Station.' *Globe and Mail*, 1954, 9.

Canavese, Peter. 'Guy Maddin – *My Winnipeg, Brand Upon the Brain!*' Groucho Reviews, http://www.grouchoreviews.com/interviews/256.

Certeau, Michel de. 'Walking in the City.' In *The Practice of Everyday Life.* 91–110. Berkeley/Los Angeles/London: University of California Press, 1984.

Church, David. 'Ode to a Nectarite Harvest.' *Bright Lights Film Journal* 58 (November 2008). <http://www.brightlightsfilm.com/58/58brain.html>

Corliss, Richard. 'Heady Brew.' *Time*, 2004. http://www.time.com/time/magazine/article/0,9171,994090,00.html

Darr, Brian. 'Guy Maddin: "I Had This Haunted Childhood."' GreenCine. https://www.greencine.com/central/guymaddin/mywinnipeg.

Deleuze, Gilles. *Cinema 2: The Time Image.* Trans. Hugh Tomlinson and Robert Galeta. Minneapolis: U of Minnesota Press, 1989.

Diones, Bruce. '*Dracula: Pages from a Virgin's Diary.*' *New Yorker*, 19 May 2003.

Dolar, Mladen. 'I Shall Be with You on Your Wedding-Night: Lacan and the Uncanny.' *October* 58 (Fall 1991): 5–24.

Donald, James. 'The City, the Cinema: Modern Spaces.' In *Visual Culture*, ed. Chris Jenks. 77–95. London/New York: Routledge, 1995.

Douglas, Edward. 'Exclusive: Guy Maddin on His Winnipeg." Crave Online. http://www.comingsoon.net/news/movienews.php?id=45772.

Douglas, Susan J. *Listening In: Radio and the American Imagination*. Minneapolis: University of Minnesota Press, 2004.

Ebert, Roger. 'The Best Films of the Decade.' *Chicago Sun-Times*. http://blogs .suntimes.com/ebert/2009/12/the_best_films_of_the_decade.html.

– 'My Winnipeg.' *Chicago Sun-Times*, 26 June 2008. <http://rogerebert.suntimes .com/apps/pbcs.dll/article?AID=/20080626/REVIEWS/644918381>

Edroso, Roy. 'Ann Savage, 1921-2008.' *Village Voice*, Monday, 29 December 2008.

Enright, Robert. 'Chicken Soup for the Stone Baby: Interrogations Towards an Elusive Autobiography.' In *Cowards Bend the Knee*, ed. Philip Monk. 129–51. Toronto: The Power Plant, 2003.

'Film Critic Top Ten Lists: 2008 Critics' Picks.' Metacritic.com. http://www .metacritic.com/film/awards/2008/toptens.shtml.

Gaonkar, Dilip Parameshwar, and Elizabeth A. Povinelli. 'Technologies of Public Forms: Circulation, Transfiguration, Recognition.' *Public Culture* 15:. 3 (2003): 385–97.

Goldie, Terry. *Fear and Temptation: The Image of the Indigene in Canadian, Australian and New Zealand Literature*. Kingston, Ont.: McGill-Queen's University Press, 1989.

Green, Renée. 'Survival: Ruminations on Archival Lacunae.' In *The Archive*, ed. Charles Merewether. 49–55. London/Cambridge, Mass.: Whitechapel/MIT Press, 2006.

Groen, Rick. *Globe and Mail*. 20 June 2008. <http://www.theglobeandmail.com/ servlet/story/RTGAM.20080620. wwinnipeg20/BNStory/Entertainment/ home>

Gunning, Tom. 'An Aesthetic of Astonishment: Early Film and the (In)Credulous Spectator.' In *Viewing Positions: Ways of Seeing Film*, ed. Linda Williams. 114–33. New Brunswick, N.J.: Rutgers University Press, 1995.

– '"Now You See It, Now You Don't": The Temporality of the Cinema of Attractions.' *The Velvet Light Trap* 32 (Fall 1993): 3–12.

Halfyard, Kurt. 'Guy Maddin Talks *My Winnipeg*, Self-Mythologizing, Psychological Honesty, and Even *the Host*.' Twitch. http://twitchfilm.net/site/view/guy-maddin-talks-up-my-winnipeg-self-mythologizing-pyschological-honesty-an/.

Hasumi, Shigehiko. 'Fiction and The "Unrepresentable": All Movies Are but Variants on the Silent Film.' *Theory, Culture & Society* 26: 2–3 (2009): 316–29.

Higgins, Dick, (with appendix by Hannah Higgins). 'Intermedia.' *Leonardo* 34: 1 (2001): 49–54.

Hoberman, Jim. 'Werner Herzog and Guy Maddin Go into Deep Freeze.' *Village Voice*. http://www.villagevoice.com/2008-06-10/film/werner-herzog-and-guy-maddin-go-into-deep-freeze.

Jameson, Fredric. 'Utopia and Failure.' Conneticut College. http://aspen.conncoll.edu/politicsandculture/page.cfm?key=18.

Jenkins, Henry. 'Transmedia Storytelling.' *Technology Review*, 15 January. 2003. http://www.technologyreview.com/biomedicine/13052/page1/.

Kennicott, Philip. 'It's Tough to Escape What Happens in "Winnipeg."' *Washington Post*. http://www.washingtonpost.com/wp-dyn/content/article/2008/06/26/AR2008062604168.html.

Kitchener-Waterloo Art Gallery. 'Online Exhibitions.' http://kwag.ca/en/exhibitions/OnlineExhibitions.asp.

Kracauer, Siegfried. *From Caligari to Hitler: A Psychological History of the German Film*. New York: Noonday Press, 1959.

Kroetsch, Robert. *The Lovely Treachery of Words: Essays Selected and New*. Studies in Canadian Literature. Toronto: Oxford University Press, 1989.

L'Atelier National du Manitoba. 'The Tragedy of the Winnipeg Jets.' Ubuweb. http://ubuweb.tumblr.com/post/134185773/latelier-national-du-manitoba-the-tragedy-of-the.

Leone, Massimo. 'Textual Wanderings: A Vertiginous Reading of W.G. Sebald.' In *W.G. Sebald: A Critical Companion*, ed. Jonathan James Long and Anne Whitehead. 89–101. Seattle: University of Washington Press, 2004.

Lim, Dennis. '*Brand Upon the Brain!*: Out of the Past.' 3–9. Criterion Collection, 2006.

mabnyc. 'Ann Savage 1921–2008.' Pass the Popcorn. http://pleasepassthepopcorn.wordpress.com/2008/12/29/ann-savage-1921-2008/.

MacDonald, Scott. 'The City as Motion Picture: Notes on Some California City Films.' *Wide Angle* 19: 4 (1997): 109–30.

Maddin, Guy. *Cowards Bend the Knee*. Edited by Philip Monk. Toronto: The Power Plant, 2003.

– *From the Atelier Tovar: Selected Writings*. Toronto: Coach House Press, 2003.

– *97 Percent True*. 51 mins. USA: Criterion Collection, 2008.

– 'My Winnipeg: An Annotated Script by Guy Maddin, Replete with Photographs, Collages, Animations and Other *My Winnipeg* Arcana.' In *My Winnipeg*, ed. Alana Wilcox 7–127. Toronto: Coach House Press, 2009.

– 'Personal Interview.' Edited by Darren Wershler. Winnipeg, 30 June 2009.

McBride, Jason. 'Brain Storm.' *Toronto Life*, 2007.

McCaffery, Steve, and bpNichol. *Rational Geomancy: The Kids of the Book-Machine: The Collected Research Reports of the Toronto Research Group, 1973–82*. Vancouver: Talonbooks, 1992.

Merewether, Charles. 'Introduction // Art and the Archive.' In *The Archive*, ed. Charles Merewether. 10–17. London/Cambridge, Mass.: Whitechapel/MIT Press, 2006.

Meyer, Moe. 'Reclaiming the Discourse of Camp.' In *Queer Cinéma: The Film Reader*, ed. Harry M. Benshoff and Sean Griffin. 137–52. New York/London: Routledge, 2004.

Miller, Toby. 'Cinema Studies Doesn't Matter; or, I Know What You Did Last Semester.' In *Keyframes: Popular Cinema and Cultural Studies*, ed. Matthew Tinkcom and Amy Villarejo. 303–11. London/New York: Routledge, 2001.

Morgenstern, Joe. "Kit Kittredge" Is a Rare Gift for Young Girls.' *Wall Street Journal*. http://online.wsj.com/article/SB121391259991589875 .html?mod=2_1168_1.

*My Winnipeg* IMDB page. 2007. <http://www.imdb.com/title/tt1093842/>

*My Winnipeg* Metacritic Page. http://www.metacritic.com/film/titles/ mywinnipeg

*My Winnipeg* Official Website. Crab Creative | Think Deeper, 2007. <http:// www.yourwinnipeg.co.uk/>

*My Winnipeg* Wikipedia Page. 7 June 2008. <http://en.wikipedia.org/wiki/ My_Winnipeg>

Nadeau, James. 'Interview with Guy Maddin, Director of *My Winnipeg*.' Big Red

& Shiny. http://www.bigredandshiny.com/cgi-bin/retrieve.pl?section=article &issue=issue86&article=INTERVIEW_WITH_GUY_1316493.

Natter, Wolfgang. ' The City as Cinematic Space: Modernism and Place in *Berlin: Symphony of a City.*' In *Place, Power, Situation, and Spectacle: A Geography of Film*, edited by Stuart C. Aitken and Leo Zonn, 203–27. Lanham: Rowman & Littlefield, 1994.

Newman, Michael. 'February 19, 1942: If Day.' *Manitoba History* 13 (Spring 1986).

Nichols, Bill. *Blurred Boundaries: Questions of Meaning in Contemporary Culture.* Bloomington/Indianapolis: Indiana University Press, 1994.

– '"Getting to Know You …": Knowledge, Power, and the Body.' In *Theorizing Documentary*, ed. Michael Renov. 174–91. New York/London: Routledge, 1993.

– *Representing Reality: Issues and Concepts in Documentary.* Bloomington: Indiana University Press, 1991.

*97 Percent True.* 51 mins. USA: Criterion Collection, 2008.

O'Donoghue, Darragh. 'Particles of Illusion: Guy Maddin and His Precursors.' *Senses of Cinema* 32 (July–September 2004). http://archive.sensesofcinema .com/contents/04/32/guy_maddin_precursors.html

O'Hehir, Andrew. 'Maddin and Herzog: Brothers of the Ice!' *Salon*, 19 June 2008. <http://www.salon.com/ent/movies/btm/feature/2008/06/19/ winnipeg/>

Ondaatje, Michael. 'Guy Maddin and Michael Ondaatje: A Conversation.' In *My Winnipeg*, ed. Alana Wilcox. 130–51. Toronto: Coach House Press, 2008.

Perloff, Marjorie. '"Vocable Scriptsigns": Differential Poetics in Kenneth Goldsmith's Fidget.' In *Fidget.* 90–107. Toronto: Coach House Press, 2000.

Persons, Dan. 'Guy Maddin Makes MY WINNIPEG Everyone's Winnipeg.' *Cinefantastique Online*, 11 June 2008. <http://cinefantastiqueonline.com/ 2008/06/11/interview-guy-maddin-makes-my-winnipeg-everyones- winnipeg/>

Peters, John Durham. *Speaking into the Air: A History of the Idea of Communication.* Chicago: University of Chicago Press, 1999.

Pinkney, Tony. 'Editor's Introduction: Modernism and Cultural Theory.' In *Politics of Modernism: Against the New Conformists*, ed. Raymond Williams. 1–29. London/New York: Verso, 2007.

Pound, Ezra. 'Paris Letter: December 1921.' *Dial* 72: 1 (1922): 73–8.

Prigge, Matt. 'Dizzy Rascal.' *Philadelphia Weekly*, 20 February 2009. http://www
.philadelphiaweekly.com/screen/39878397.html

Rossellini, Isabella. *In the Name of the Father, the Daughter and the Holy Spirits.*
Munich: Schirmer/Mosel, 2006.

Schivelbusch, Wolfgang. *The Railway Journey: The Industrialization and Perception of
Time and Space in the 19th Century.* New ed. Berkeley: University of California
Press, 1986.

Sconce, Jeffrey. *Haunted Media: Electronic Presence from Telegraphy to Television*,
Console-Ing Passions. Durham, N.C.: Duke University Press, 2000.

Scott, A.O. 'Permafrost Makes the Heart Grow Stranger in a Haunted
Snow Globe.' *New York Times.* http://movies.nytimes.com/2008/06/13/
movies/13winn.html.

Sedgwick, Eve Kosofsky. *Between Men: English Literature and Male Homosocial Desire*,
Gender and Culture. New York: Columbia University Press, 1985.

Seguin, Denis. 'Winnipeg, Mon Amour.' *Walrus*, January/February 2008.
http://www.walrusmagazine.com/articles/2008.02-film-guy-maddin-my-
winnipeg/

Seitz, Matt Zoller. 'Funny Guy: Maddin's Masterpiece Goes Meta.' *New York
Press*, 2004.

Shaviro, Steven. 'Fire and Ice: The Films of Guy Maddin.' In *North of Everything:
English-Canadian Cinema since 1980*, ed. William Beard and Jerry White. 216–21.
Edmonton: University of Alberta Press, 2002.

– 'My Winnipeg.' *The Pinnochio Theory*, 15 July 2008.<http://www.shaviro.com/
Blog/?p=650>

Smetanka, Andy. 'Cold Throbbings: How I Stalked Guy Maddin.' In *My Winnipeg*, ed. Alana Wilcox. 166–72. Toronto: Coach House Press, 2009.

'Soda Pictures Theatrical Press Kit: *My Winnipeg*.' Edited by Soda Pictures. 9.
London, 2008.

Sorrento, Matthew. '*My Winnipeg*.' *Film Threat*, 22 June 2008. <http://www
.filmthreat.com/index.php?section=reviews&Id=11006>

Spieker, Sven. *The Big Archive: Art from Bureaucracy.* Cambridge, Mass.: MIT Press,
2008.

Strathausen, Carsten. 'Uncanny Spaces: The City in Ruttmann and Vertov.' In
*Screening the City*, ed. Mark Shiel and Tony Fitzmaurice. 15–40. London/New
York: Verso, 2003.

Straw, Will. 'The Circulatory Turn.' In *The Wireless Spectrum: The Politics, Practices and Poetics of Mobile Media*, ed. Barbara Crow, Michael Longford. and Kim Sawchuk. Toronto: University of Toronto Press, 2009.

– 'Reinhabiting Lost Languages: Guy Maddin's *Careful*.' In *Canada's Best Features: Critical Essays on 15 Canadian Films*, ed. Eugene P. Walz. 304–18. Amsterdam, NY: Rodopi, 2002.

Sullivan, Nikki. *A Critical Introduction to Queer Theory*. Edinburgh: Edinburgh University Press, 2003.

Toles, George E. 'From Archangel to Mandragora in Your Own Back Yard; Collaborating with Guy Maddin.' In *A House Made of Light*. Detroit: Wayne State University Press, 2001.

Toles, George, and Guy Maddin. 'Dikemaster's Daughter.' *Border Crossings* 16: 4 (1997): 34–41.

Varga, Darrell. 'Desire in Bondage: Guy Maddin's *Careful*.' *Canadian Journal of Film Studies* 8: 2 (1998): 56–70.

Vatnsdal, Caelum. *Kino Delirium: The Films of Guy Maddin*. Winnipeg: Arbeiter Ring, 2000.

– 'Strange Direction.' In *My Winnipeg*, ed. Alana Wilcox. 179–88. Toronto: Coach House Press, 2009.

Wershler-Henry, Darren. 'Return from Without: Louis Riel and Liminal Space.' In *Gone to Croatan: Origins of North American Dropout Culture*, ed. Ron Sakolsky and James Koehnline. 315–28. Brooklyn, N.Y.: Autonomedia/AK Press, 1993.

– 'Strangled by an Intestine!' *Virus* 23: $ (1992): 11–14.

Wigon, Zachary. 'Tribeca Film Festival 2008: "You Can't Cheat Documentary": A Conversation with Guy Maddin.' The House Next Door. http://www.thehousenextdooronline.com/2008/04/tribeca-film-festival-2008-you-cant.html.

Williams, Raymond. *The Country and the City*. Frogmore: St Albans, 1975.

– *Marxism and Literature*, Marxist Introductions. Oxford/New York: Oxford University Press, 1977.

Woloski, Jason. 'Guy Maddin.' http://archive.sensesofcinema.com/contents/directors/03/maddin.html.

Youngblood, Gene. *Expanded Cinema*. 1st ed. New York/Toronto: P. Dutton / Clarke, Irwin, 1970.

Žižek, Slavoj. *Enjoy Your Symptom!: Jacques Lacan in Hollywood and Out.* 2nd ed. New York/London: Routledge, 2001.
– *For They Know Not What They Do : Enjoyment as a Political Factor.* 2nd ed. Radical Thinkers. London /New York: Verso, 2008.
– *On Belief.* Thinking in Action. New York/London: Routledge, 2001.
– *Organs without Bodies: On Deleuze and Consequences.* New York/London: Routledge, 2004.
– *The Parallax View.* Short Circuits. Cambridge, Mass./London: MIT Press, 2006.
– *The Plague of Fantasies.* London/New York: Verso, 1997.
– *The Sublime Object of Ideology.* London/New York: Verso, 1989.
– *Tarrying with the Negative: Kant, Hegel, and the Critique of Ideology.* Post-Contemporary Interventions. Durham, N.C.: Duke University Press, 1993.